"This is not a book; it is a timeless masterpiece to be savored for generations. If you want to truly find the missing deep dream of your life, this practical piece of literary work will help you discover it. From inspirational advice to life stories that will hold your interest for hours, Dr. Castleberry makes you want to get up off the couch and become the next deep-dream success story."

— DAVID BRODY, chief political correspondent,
Christian Broadcasting Network

"Dr. Castleberry has written a book of remarkable clarity and insight. He shows us that discovering one's deep dream is the key that unlocks our true potential and enables us to achieve the deep sense of fulfillment God intends for each and every one of us."

— ROB MCKENNA, attorney general, Washington

"Dr. Joseph Castleberry has written a book that gives readers a powerful alternative to the white-picket-fence future that compels so many Americans. The book's lively narrative style frames its insightful message: 'There is a clear plan for your life; don't miss it.' Buy copies for every dream seeker you know."

— CARLOS CAMPO, PhD, president, Regent University

"This book offers a solid guide to true fulfillment through a combination of inspiring stories, biblical principles, and fresh insights, all presented in simple but sparkling language that is a delight to the reader."

— GEORGE WOOD, general superintendent, Assemblies of God

"Living with a sense of mission and purpose is the key to seeing dreams become realities. In *Your Deepest Dream*, Joseph Castleberry explores what it takes to realize the fullest expression of your God-given potential. Daydream no longer—an exciting journey awaits you!"

— JOHN LINDELL, lead pastor, James River Assembly, Ozark, Missouri

"Being driven is only half of the solution to success. Joe Castleberry masterfully presents the other half: being guided by your deepest dream. This book helped me to adjust my compass heading so that I was on the correct course to true success."

— COURT DURKALSKI, CEO/servant, Truline Industries, Inc.;
author of *Winning at Work*

"Dr. Joe Castleberry has hit a grand slam with *Your Deepest Dream*. Of the seven billion people on the planet, most haven't yet experienced the meaning and purpose for their lives — they're simply existing. This book not only challenges us to identify the deep dream in our lives but also shows us how to live it through right thinking, inspirational stories, and solid biblical principles. Discover your deep dream and make it reality!"

— SCOTT MCCHRYSTAL, U.S. Army, retired;
former chaplain of the United States Military Academy, West Point

YOUR DEEPEST DREAM

Discovering God's True Vision
for Your Life

JOSEPH CASTLEBERRY

NAVPRESS
Discipleship Inside Out®

Discipleship Inside Out®

NavPress is the publishing ministry of The Navigators, an international Christian organization and leader in personal spiritual development. NavPress is committed to helping people grow spiritually and enjoy lives of meaning and hope through personal and group resources that are biblically rooted, culturally relevant, and highly practical.

For a free catalog go to www.NavPress.com
or call 1.800.366.7788 in the United States or 1.800.839.4769 in Canada.

ISBN-13: 978-1-61521-826-4

Cover design by Arvid Wallen
Cover image by Shutterstock

Some of the anecdotal illustrations in this book are true to life and are included with the permission of the persons involved. All other illustrations are composites of real situations, and any resemblance to people living or dead is coincidental.

Unless otherwise identified, all Scripture quotations in this publication are taken from The Holy Bible, English Standard Version (ESV), copyright © 2001 by Crossway Bibles, a division of Good News Publishers. Used by permission. All rights reserved. The other version used is the *Holy Bible, New International Version*® (NIV®), copyright © 1973, 1978, 1984 by Biblica, used by permission of Zondervan, all rights reserved.

Castleberry, Joseph Lee.
  Your deepest dream : discovering God's true vision for your life /
Joseph L. Castleberry.
    p. cm.
  Includes bibliographical references.
  ISBN 978-1-61521-826-4
  1. Dreams--Religious aspects--Christianity. 2. Christian life. 3.
Vocation--Christianity. I. Title.
  BR115.D74C37 2012
  248.2'9--dc23
                                        2011030985

Printed in the United States of America

1 2 3 4 5 6 7 8 / 16 15 14 13 12

To the late James Jackson Castleberry,
my irreplaceable dream dad.

and to Ray Noah, may
God speak to you as
you read.

Joseph

CONTENTS

CHAPTER 1

DEEP DREAMS

It is the birthright of college students to complain about cafeteria food. But Randy Borman, a student at Michigan State University, was eating from a board plan that would make any red-blooded American complain. Supporting himself on the fruits of a meager income from factory work and occasional urban hunting trips (hunting rabbits and pigeons with a pellet gun and seeking fresh roadkill), he became fed up with his life as an underfed college student.[1] Although he was blessed with a brilliant intellect and deeply appreciated the insights and strengths of Western culture, he knew the American Dream was not his dream. So he dropped out of school and moved to Ecuador to join a Stone Age Amazonian Indian tribe.

Randy was going home. Born in 1955 to missionary parents in Ecuador, he had grown up in the jungle. His family lived with the Cofan, learning their language and customs in order to translate the Bible into the Cofan language. They not only introduced the people to the gospel, but they also cared about the Cofan's physical needs. Randy grew up learning the ways of the jungle, hunting with a blowgun, wearing tribal clothing, living off the land.

What he found when he returned to the Cofan in 1974 was an endangered people group. Everyone has heard of endangered animal species. But most people are unaware that human diversity is highly endangered all over the world because of the march of globalization and urbanization. Between 50 and 90 percent of the six thousand languages spoken in the world today may pass into extinction by the end of this century.[2] The people groups who once spoke them will have blended into the national cultures around them. Their ways of understanding the world, their cultures, their wisdom will all go away with them. The Cofan tribe, reduced to just a few hundred members, was well on its way to extinction.

The main reason for the looming extinction of the Cofan, Randy discovered, was the increasing destruction of their tribal lands in the jungle. First a U.S.-based oil company and later the nationalized Ecuadorian oil company had discovered oil, built roads into the jungle, and begun to extract it. As they worked, they were destroying the rain forest.

The Cofan were forced to leave their oil-fouled homes, and as they left the jungle, they were being reduced to poverty and forced to look for Western-style employment. A beautiful people and a beautiful way of life were being lost. It does not take a lot of sense to realize that is a bad thing. But for Randy it was personal. His home was being destroyed, along with the people and culture he loved.

Armed with his Western education and a deep knowledge of the jungle, the Cofan, and their culture, Randy began the campaign that would become his deep dream. Rather than eke out an unhappy living in the United States to achieve a form of prosperity that didn't appeal to him, he would become one of the Cofan and spend the rest of his life fighting for the survival of their way of life. He married a Cofan woman and had children, committing himself to live his whole life in the jungle.

While more and more Cofan were leaving their people to seek employment among the dominant Ecuadorian society, Randy went the other way. He led a small group of Cofan deep into the jungle, where they started a new settlement called Zabalo.

After establishing a village to serve as the new home of the Cofan, Randy convinced the Ecuadorian government to set aside a million acres of rain forest as a national ecological park (like Yellowstone National Park in the United States). There, his family and friends could continue to live the rich life of their Cofan ancestors, at harmony with the jungle and each other. But unfortunately, ever since Adam and Eve were expelled from Eden, human beings have found it hard to sustain paradise. It was not long before the oil company found them and began experimental drilling.

Randy was determined not to let his home be destroyed. While the whole story is too long to tell here, and it isn't over yet, the long and short of the matter is that Randy became the "Gringo Chief" of the Zabalo Cofan.[3] His simple dream of returning to his idyllic boyhood life in the jungle had deepened into the dream of leading the Zabalo Cofan in a sacred mission, fulfilling their destiny as protectors of the rain forest. As he discovered that deep dream, it took him deeper into the jungle and took the jungle deeper into him. In the process, he became a moral hero.

Randy knows that the West is not all bad, and he has continued to stay on top of the best developments in Western technology. His political action (and sometimes armed resistance) has forced the Ecuadorian government to fund a school and a strong Internet connection in Zabalo. The Cofan children go to school part of the day and spend the rest of the day getting a priceless education: They are learning languages—English, French, and German, as well as the Cofan language—and they really do need them. Through Randy's networking with foreign businesses, they work as guides for a booming ecotourism business, serving the many foreigners who want to visit the unspoiled paradise where they live.

Seeking partners both inside and outside Ecuador, Randy has set up eco-friendly forest product businesses that create the income his people need to participate in the miraculous benefits of modernity while ensuring the survival of the forest long into the future. The Cofan have become a thoroughly postmodern indigenous people. To the uninformed Westerner looking at their pictures, they may look like seminaked jungle savages. To those who know the rest of the story, they are one of the most sophisticated, up-to-the-minute people groups in the world.

For his efforts, Randy has received just about every environmentalist award the West has to offer. He is widely recognized as a great man, and he deserves a Nobel Peace Prize for his work. And did I mention that Randy and the Cofan are Christians? Randy's parents were missionaries, and he keeps a close relationship with his missionary brother who lives in a less protected part of the jungle. But Randy is not a missionary. He is the CEO of a postmodern Indian tribe. He says, "Everyone wants to excel in the West, to define themselves by being the best at something specific. . . . I've got something . . . no one else is trying to excel at—saving a forest and leading a group of indigenous people."[4]

Randy Borman is what I would call a successful dreamer. Not only has he dreamed, but he has allowed his dream to mature in ways that have inspired him to achieve real depth in his life. Unfortunately, many people are not successful dreamers. Their dreams have either died or never been developed.

According to Henry David Thoreau, most people "lead lives of quiet desperation."[5] If he was right, I believe it is because human beings—all seven billion–plus of us who live today—are unique, irreplaceable souls with a divine destiny to fulfill. No two of us are exactly alike, even identical twins who share the same genetic makeup. Yet society often has a way of trying to force us to be and act and live alike, following the tracks of what is expected of us by others, crushing our individual souls the way smokers snuff out cigarette butts with the soles of their shoes.

I mentioned the genetic makeup of twins. Makeup—now there's a concept. We all have a genetic makeup and a unique potential and destiny. But often, rather than making up a future that looks like us, we "put on makeup," desperately trying to make ourselves fit into the expectations of others—our parents, our peers, even our enemies.

Rather than fit into other people's expectations of him, Randy Borman imagined a future that would truly fulfill him, and he bravely set out to make it a reality. If he had not dared to dream a unique dream for himself, he could never have established and maintained the Zabalo community. His people would now be virtually extinct. He'd be living an unfulfilled life far from the rain forest rather than the hunting/fishing/philosophy-reading/technology-adopting/airplane-flying post-modern jungle life he now loves. So much would have been lost. I'm so glad he found his dream and had the courage to live it.

I call the dream that will most perfectly fulfill each of us our *deep dream*. Not everyone's deep dream will be as dramatic as Randy Borman's. Very few will become famous or rich or great in the eyes of society. But I believe God has a unique and special deep dream for each one of us, and when we find and embrace our God-given dream, we will find the greatest possible fulfillment.

Throughout this book, we will explore goals, dreams, destiny, and success. People conceive goals and dreams in different ways, but I want to offer my own clear definitions here because being confused about them can gravely interfere with our ability to conceive our deepest dream. Goals are simple objectives we can achieve by hard work and persistence. Dreams are deeper, more complex objectives that require more than just our hard work. Because they are big-picture aspirations, dreams require a measure of what we sometimes call luck—what Christians call the favor or grace of God. For example, if you dream of being president of the United States, you not only need to work hard for a long time and succeed at lots of smaller personal goals, but you also need "things to go right for you." Factors outside yourself have to conspire to put you in the right place at the right time to make such a dream come true.

The uncertainty of such dreams often leads us to fantasize or daydream about them. Some people fall into the trap of daydreaming about their dreams and never doing the work it takes to achieve them. Living that way leads to frustration and failure. Still other people not only work hard, but also see their circumstances cooperate to help them fulfill their dreams. But fulfilling such dreams will not necessarily make them "fulfilled people."

True fulfillment comes when we discover the overarching deep dream God intends for us. That dream involves goals, dreams, destiny (which I will explain later), and the development of moral character. It is the dream that, when discovered, will wake us up from either a life of aimless confusion or a life of confused aiming.

Have you noticed that in night dreams our actions are often confusing and based on half-baked ideas? Things more or less make sense in the dream, but they don't always fit together very well. Unfortunately, many people live their lives as if they were dreaming, asleep at the wheel — not really sure where they are going, but speeding toward whatever is up ahead. No wonder Thoreau called it "quiet desperation."

This book calls on you to wake up from daydreaming and to commit yourself to a deep dream. People who have discovered their deep dream find a sense of mission in life. They know where they are going, and the goals and dreams they pursue combine with a sense of destiny, giving their lives meaning and purpose. They are truly alert, truly awake. They understand the will of God for their lives and live in a sense of profound enthusiasm — even though their lives, like everyone else's, involve struggles, contradictions, and disappointments. But even in the midst of those things, they have discovered the deepest meaning of their lives.

The poet E. E. Cummings is perhaps most famous for the fact that people stopped using capital letters to write his name. That is a pretty shallow thing to be famous for, but his poetry was hardly shallow. (Cummings himself preferred the capital letters.) In one of his poems, he wrote, "dive for dreams/or a slogan may topple you."[6] Cummings seemed to understand that if people are going to be successful in achieving their dreams, they have to live deeply. Slogans are the exact opposite of deep thinking. They are gross oversimplifications, useful for marketing, but not deep enough to sustain a human dream. If you are going to find the dream that will fulfill you, you will have to dive deep.

In this book, I will tell stories about men and women from all over the world who have discovered their deep dreams. I'll share wisdom from the Bible and other sources, as well as some of the things I've observed as a dreamer myself. But the main thing I hope you will do as you read is discover the God-given dream that will help you make the most of your life.

I believe that a deep dream must be an innate expression of who you are and who you must become if you are to realize all your potential as a human being created in God's image. For that reason, each chapter focuses on an aspect of deep character and identity that is present in people who reach their greatest potential and live out their deep dreams. As you read, be sure to do the exercises at the end of each chapter. They will help you develop these qualities in yourself. Maybe you have never read a book that way before, but this book is going to require you to interact with it. I think you will be glad you did. Read on! You are about to dive deep. As you do, you will discover great things!

CHAPTER 2

KNOW YOURSELF

The ancient Greek oracle of Delphi taught that the greatest wisdom was to "know yourself." That little phrase is a serious mouthful of good advice, because a person who does not know himself or herself does not really know anything. Unless we know ourselves, we can never really know our neighbors, and we cannot know God. We can have encounters with people or with God. We can begin a relationship with others or with God. But we will never advance far in any relationship unless we figure out who we are and what our life means.

When I was growing up in the 1960s and 1970s, many people were breaking out of conventional restraints in order to "find themselves." They became hippies. They talked about escaping from the rat race. They talked about sexual revolution and women's liberation. They talked about mind-expanding drugs and psychedelic experiences. People were getting into "transactional analysis" in an effort to find their "inner child." These various efforts at self-discovery were sometimes disastrous, sometimes more or less successful, depending on what people did. Those who tried to find their authentic selves through drugs or sexual experimentation made little or no progress. Many only succeeded in becoming remarkably egotistical. As the young people of that period grew older, some social scientists called them the Me Generation.

After the 1970s, it seemed that many people had either found themselves or given up on the search. So, in the 1980s the majority of people decided it was time to start seeking money rather than their authentic selves; so much for "know yourself." I'll leave it to the generations of the nineties and afterward to write their own stories instead of trying to chart them out here. All I will say about the current generation of college-age students — sometimes called Millennials — is that my children belong to that generation, so it is far and away my favorite. I am likely to have grandchildren in the next generation, so I am going to like that one also. In any case, people throughout history have struggled to know themselves, and I'm sure this book will be as relevant to my future grandchildren as it is to people today.

One of the outstanding qualities of the biblical character Joseph of Egypt was that he had a clear sense of himself. He was one of the greatest dreamers in history. His story has inspired millions of people across the millennia. In our time, major films and Broadway shows have been produced about Joseph's dreams and their fulfillment, about how he began life as a favorite son who dreamed of leading his family in honor, only to be sold into slavery by his jealous brothers. But no matter how grim his story became, Joseph never gave up on the dreams God gave him during childhood, and in the end he achieved unparalleled success, achievement, prosperity, and power. (If you don't know his story, you may want to read it in the Bible, in Genesis 37–50.)

In the Aramaic culture of the ancient Middle East, people believed that a person's name was a prophecy about his or her true character. They believed a name could tell you a lot about a person, and it was an embarrassing thing if you did not live up to your good name. (On the other hand, parents would sometimes give a child a bad name, creating the opposite effect. Those children would spend the rest of their lives trying to *live down* their names.)

Joseph's name meant "he prospers," and indeed, his God-given mission in life led him to great prosperity. His story is that of a man who fulfilled his true nature. Joseph prospered in everything he did. He did not let adversity and setbacks and enemies make him a stagnant, bitter person. Every time he got knocked down, he popped back up. As a child, he prospered. As a slave, he prospered. As a prisoner, he prospered. As a friend, he prospered. As a son, he prospered. And finally, as the manager of the known world in a time of famine and drought, he prospered.

Joseph lived up to his name because he had a deep sense of himself. He knew who he was, and he knew what his dream was. He knew he was destined for leadership and honor, and he never let his external circumstances strip him of his dignity. If he was to be a slave, he would be nobler than his master. If he was to be a prisoner, he would be the freest person in the jail. If he was to be hated, he would give back understanding. If he was to be attacked, he would respond in mercy. At the end of his life, his whole family bowed before him in honor and gratitude for saving their lives.

Joseph's persistence in spite of oppression reminds me of the story of Viktor Frankl, a Holocaust survivor who became a famous psychotherapist. He told about what it was like to completely lose control over his external surroundings. Facing the incredible brutality of the Nazis in a concentration camp, he began to hate them for their cruelty. As he fed on that hatred, he began to hate himself.

After a while, he came to understand that the Nazis were not defeating him by controlling his circumstances. They were defeating him by controlling his interior life. This discovery led him to a profound and life-changing truth: While you cannot control your external circumstances, you can control how you respond to them. In his book *Man's Search for Meaning*, Frankl says, "Everything can be taken from a man but . . . the last of the human freedoms — to choose one's attitude in any given set of circumstances."[1] Frankl realized that once he gained control over his inner life, the Nazis would never be able to defeat him. Even if they killed his body, they would not be able to defeat his spirit.

One of the reasons it is so important to know yourself is that you can never exercise self-control over your responses to life's circumstances until you do. To develop self-control, you need to know your own inner nature and the source of it. You need to know your strengths and the wells they spring from. You need to know your weaknesses and the cracks they ooze from. Finally, you must know your deep dream and learn to draw inspiration and motivation from those peaks on the horizon ahead of you.

Let's look a bit more closely at each of these.

1. Know your own inner nature and the source of it. There is simply no way to achieve this without spending time in reflection and deep thought about yourself. What are your strengths? What do you love? What would you do if you could do anything you wanted, and why would you want to do it? What is your deepest regret and why?

Be aware that there are pitfalls in this important activity. Some people begin to ask these kinds of questions, take one look at their inward reflection, and are so horrified that they resolve never to look in that mirror again. This tactic is a guaranteed formula for spectacular failure in life. Socrates said it well some three hundred years before the birth of Christ: "The unexamined life is not worth living." If you refuse to take a good look at your inner self regularly, you will lose control of your life. Either other people will control you, or habits and substances will control you. This ignoble way of life is unworthy of a human being created in the image and likeness of God.

On the other hand, some people become utterly paralyzed because they cannot stop thinking about themselves. The Greek myth of Narcissus tells the story of a young man who was so fascinated with his own reflection in a pool of water that he gazed at himself uncontrollably. Eventually he pined away and died. Few things are as destructive as excessive contemplation of one's own self. In memory of the Narcissus story, psychologists call this personality disorder "narcissism."

Between these two extremes, you must find the proper balance of self-examination and activity in the world. It takes courage to look deeply at one's self, and many people fall victim to cowardice and live a life not worth living. It also takes courage to take a good look at the world and engage in the tasks of life and relationships with other people. But self-examination and self-knowledge are crucial for identifying and achieving your deep dream.

Self-examination must also include knowledge of the source of your life and identity. There are essentially two points of view on this issue. Naturalists — people with the view that there is nothing in the cosmos except nature, and thus no God — believe that the source of your life is blind luck. Under this view, you are a random combination of genes passed down by nature from your ancestors, who themselves were the product of an incredibly lucky series of mutations from other forms of life that by chance happened to become a living cell in the midst of some proto-organic ooze. This combination of lucky genes is, in this view, enhanced by circumstances and by choices you make.

The other major position on the source of life and identity is the theistic one, in which God is understood to be our Creator. In Genesis 1, the biblical story of creation goes along in prose until it reaches its climax, the creation of human beings. At that point, the story bursts into poetry—even song—like an old-fashioned musical. It sings out that we were created in the image and likeness of God, male and female alike. That makes us more special than anything else in all creation. It tells us that our true identity is to be sons and daughters of God.

I believe that until we come to see our true identity, we can never fully understand who we are. Most people live as estranged children of God who never really talk to God and certainly never hear his voice. Anyone who has lived this kind of silent or one-way relationship with their earthly parents knows it is no way to live. The same is true of our relationship with God.

When we have owned our identity as God's children, we naturally want to relate to God on a speaking basis. That is what prayer is all about. Prayer is nothing more than conversation with God. True prayer is a two-way conversation with God. If you do not pray—and by far, most Americans do pray—or if your prayers have never been a matter of God speaking back to you, I want to tell you that God really does speak to people. One of the most important ways God speaks to us is by giving us direction for our lives, telling us who we are, and giving us a dream to pursue.

Because I'm always talking about God speaking to me, people often ask me what that is like. Over the course of my life, I have sought to discern what God wanted me to do before making any major decision, and the Lord has spoken to me in all kinds of ways. The basis for this is the fact that I am always talking to God! God then responds in all kinds of ways.

First of all, God has spoken richly in the Scriptures. I often get a clear sense of direction about issues or projects through immersing myself in the Bible. The Holy Spirit causes the words of Scripture to leap in my mind, so to speak. Hebrews 4:12 says, "The word of God is living and active, sharper than any two-edged sword, piercing to the division of soul and spirit . . . and discerning the thoughts and intentions of the heart." I know from experience just how true that is!

Sometimes God's voice to me is a sense of peace about what I want to do, giving me encouragement to move forward. Sometimes when I am in prayer, a fresh thought comes out of nowhere that I instantly recognize as God speaking to me. Sometimes I awake from sleep with a pounding thought — like the time when I was about to start my doctoral degree at a particular university and I woke up in the middle of the night with a question hammering in my head: "When did I tell you to go to X university?" I changed course immediately!

At other times, people have been the voice of God to me — like the time Doug Oss essentially prophesied to me that within months I would get a call to be president of Northwest University. It was a crazy idea, as Northwest already had a wonderful president. But God was speaking to me through Doug, and just a few months later his prophecy came true. Sometimes God's voice takes the form of circumstantial break-throughs that give us clear direction. Once I even saw graffiti on a wall in Ecuador that made me know God's will for me.

Some people inevitably will conclude that all of this

communication from God to me is just my imagination at work. If so, I thank God for my imagination! It has led me into every great decision I've ever made. In George Bernard Shaw's play *Saint Joan*, Joan of Arc is being persecuted by her captors, who mock her claim that God has spoken to her. They say, "That's only your imagination"—to which Joan responds, "I know; that is how God speaks to me."[2] The same is true for me.

It would take a whole book for me to tell you about all the ways God has spoken to me personally and to other people today and throughout history. But the most important advice I can give you is this: If you have not established a talking relationship with God, do it soon. God talks to people who are listening and keeps talking to people who obey. Talking with God will have an enormous impact on your ability to pursue and fulfill your dreams.

2. Know your strengths and their limits. If you do not, you will never be able to reach your peak levels of performance. You will never be great at anything unless you dedicate yourself to doing the things you are really good at.

When I was in high school, I had a number of interests and talents. One of the things that most gave me satisfaction was music. I was a tuba and string bass player in the band, and I worked hard to be a good musician. Because at that time in my life I got more self-esteem from music than from anything else, I decided to make an effort to become a professional musician and symphony orchestra player.

When I went to college, I worked hard to achieve this goal. I played the tuba eight hours a day for much of my first year. I was proud of dedicating so much time to my instrument, but as a people person, I got more and more miserable in doing it. Finally an event happened that changed my life.

The tuba chair (there is only one) in the Boston Symphony opened up. Three hundred fifty tuba players — the best unseated players in the world, as well as many established musicians from less prestigious orchestras — tried out for that one chair. When I read about this, I began to do some realistic reflection.

When you are spending eight hours a day on an instrument, you discover the limits of your talent. I was finding my limits. The same lack of eye-hand coordination that made me a mediocre athlete was showing up in my musical endeavors and limiting me there as well. I took a hard look at myself and decided that while I might possibly be one of the top ten collegiate tuba players in the state of Alabama, I was probably never going to be one of the top five hundred players in the country. My prospects for a decent career as a symphony player seemed pretty dismal. Even if I did become one of the top five hundred players, that wasn't even going to get me a tryout for a major symphony orchestra position. I would never even be one of the also-rans.

Faced with this reality, I decided to change majors. I realized that my early childhood calling to become a minister was what I should dedicate myself to pursuing. So, I changed my major and moved to a different college. I have thanked God a thousand times that I became a minister rather than a musician. While I'll always enjoy making music, that is not my greatest strength. If I had not figured out what my greatest strengths are, and if I had not determined the limits of my strengths, I would have been doomed to a mediocre life. Make sure you figure out your strengths and their limits.

Not only do you need to know your strengths, you need to understand the wells that they spring from. In general, everyone should understand that strengths well up in our lives from our parents and family, our friends and associates, and from

God who has made us for a purpose.

As a young person, I knew that I had inherited my musical abilities from my parents. My mother came from a line of musically talented people, and my father's grandfather had been a songwriter and singing-school teacher. Much of the development of my musical talents came from friends who had connected me to the right teachers, and from my parents who paid for expensive lessons. But the real source of that strength came from God, who had a particular purpose in giving me those talents. If I had only paid attention to parents and friends, I would likely have continued to be a musician. The fact that I yielded that talent to God in the end made it possible for that strength — with all its limitations — to be expressed as a small part of my overall calling to be a minister, scholar, and educator. Had I continued trying to develop that strength without reference to its ultimate source, I would have failed to find out the real meaning of that gift and would have used it improperly.

When we realize our strengths come to us from others, it gives us a basis for proper humility. We come to see that no one deserves all the credit for his or her strengths. We owe so much to the genetic and environmental gifts our parents give us, and we owe much of what is left over to friends, associates, teachers, and others who influence us. All personal achievements are in large measure social achievements.

When we realize that God is the ultimate source of our strengths, we can realize that we also owe a debt to God. Only God knows how our combination of strengths should work together for the fulfillment of our true purpose in life. Giving God the credit for our strengths and achievements keeps the springs of strength from getting plugged up by arrogance and pride. It guarantees a continual flow of strength and helps us move forward in achieving our dreams.

3. *Know your character weaknesses and the cracks they ooze from.* It is often said that our weaknesses tend to be the flip side of our strengths. This is a great truth. Many of our weaknesses are not things in themselves, but rather corruptions of our strengths. Weaknesses do not spring up like wells, but rather they leak out through cracks. In other words, weaknesses are not what you are; they are imperfections related to what you are.

I once knew a man who was a skilled storyteller. He could talk—and keep the attention of others—for hours. This was his greatest strength. But there was a crack in his character. He was an incorrigible liar. I often thought, when catching him in a lie, that he did not even know when he was lying. He would become so engrossed in his own creativity that he couldn't tell the difference between his reality and his fictions. Obviously, this tendency to lie was a crack in the wall of his strength.

The truth is that we all have weaknesses in our character. No one is "nothing but wall." The difference between people who achieve a fulfilling dream and live it out for the rest of their lives and people who either fail to achieve their dreams or achieve them only for a short time is simple. Those who live out a dream all their lives are constantly repairing the cracks of weakness in the walls of their strength. They consistently examine themselves to see where their character may be leaking, and they do whatever is necessary to bolster their character and prevent a leak from destroying their walls. Don't let your dreams collapse just because you refuse to fortify your character.

Building character has little to do with making a resolution to stop failing. It involves setting up a barrier between yourself and failure. An example comes from a man I know who is a very handsome guy. He travels a lot and speaks publicly to various groups. He always talks about how great his wife is and how much he loves her. The genuineness of his love is transparent. As a result, other women are discouraged from flirting with him, and he avoids temptation when he is out traveling. His public display of dedication to his wife bolsters the wall of his strength.

No matter what people's weaknesses are, there are ways to strengthen their character and integrity. It only takes some thought and careful attention. Of course, everyone should reflect daily on what to do to decrease their chances of failure in life.

4. Know your deep dream and learn to draw inspiration and motivation from those peaks that stand on the horizon ahead of you. Without a doubt, you will face many discouraging moments in the course of fulfilling your deep dream.

Imagine how discouraging it was for Jesus the day before his crucifixion. The New Testament tells us how he had lived a righteous life serving the people around him. His deep dream was to declare and demonstrate the kingdom of God on earth, healing the sick, setting free those who were captive to evil, and finally, dying on the cross for the sins of humanity. As he faced the end, he had been terribly whipped and tortured, and he struggled to carry the cross up to the hill where he was to be unjustly executed as a criminal.

How did he keep moving forward? In Hebrews 12:2, the Bible says that "for the joy set before him [Jesus] endured the cross, scorning its shame, and sat down at the right hand of the throne of God" (NIV). As Jesus went through the most difficult moments of his life, he kept thinking about the end results of his dream. He knew the results of his suffering would be the redemption of humanity, his resurrection from the dead, and the final moment of triumph when he would sit on heaven's throne with God. Jesus knew that God would not fail, and the thought of his future victory was enough to get him through the times when his circumstances seemed to contradict his dream.

Just like Jesus, we need to keep our eyes on the prize. While deep dreams are not fragile and can often survive despite years of frustration, it is a great inspiration to meditate periodically on what you are striving for. Take time to meditate on what the fulfillment of your deep dream is going to mean for you and the people you love.

GO DEEPER

This and each of the following chapters have exercises to help you consider what you need to know and do to fulfill your deep dream. Because you will be writing down some very private thoughts, you should get a notebook or diary for your responses. If you write down private things in this book, be sure not to give it away!

.1. Develop a habit of spending about fifteen minutes a day in reflection about your life. This habit will be even more effective if you will direct that contemplation toward God and ask him to show you things about your life and activities. Be sure to celebrate successes and think about how to repeat them. You should also consider failings and how to avoid them. This reflection may sometimes be uncomfortable, but you will find it causes you to live a much more fruitful life.

2. Make an inventory of your five greatest strengths. Afterward, talk to several close friends. Without sharing your list with them, ask them what they think your five greatest strengths are. Then compare their lists with yours. Anything

they listed that you left out needs further consideration. Ask them why they think you are strong in that area. If you listed things they did not list, ask them why they did not include those things on their lists. If your friends are honest with you, it will help you discover weaknesses you were not aware of, as well as bringing to your attention strengths you may have overlooked.

3. Taking your consolidated list of strengths, consider whether the activities you are currently involved in take full advantage of those strengths. Does your current job or study program allow you to use your best strengths? If not, you may need to consider a change that will allow you to pursue your dream more directly.

4. Make three columns on a sheet of paper. Write a list of your worst failings and weaknesses in column 1. In column 2, relate these weaknesses to your strengths, and consider how they relate to cracks in your character. In the third column, think about what safeguards you can build in your life to avoid falling into temptation, weakness, or failings.

CHAPTER 3

KNOW GOD

The gospel of Luke tells the story of Zacchaeus, a man who absolutely was not living up to his name. Zacchaeus means "righteous man." But Zacchaeus was anything but that. Even though he was a Jew, he was a chief tax collector for the Roman Empire, helping to oppress his own people. He had become rich by overcharging them for their taxes. Because he had the full imperial might of the Roman army behind him, it was hard for others to stand up to him.

The Jews of Jericho hated Zacchaeus. Every time they spoke his name, they must have said to themselves, "Yeah, right. Righteous man. What a joke." Zacchaeus was what we would call a sycophant of the Romans. *Sycophant* is an uncommon English word meaning "servile flatterer," "toady," or "flunky." A sycophant does someone else's dirty work to try to gain approval. The people of Jerusalem—who often spoke Greek because it was the trade language of the Roman Empire—would have used that word in its original form, *sycophantes*, to refer to Zacchaeus, but it would have had a slightly different meaning. In Greek, *sycophantes* literally means "fig-revealer" or "fig-shaker." A *sycophantes* was originally a person who shook fig trees so that the figs would fall to the ground and thus be seen for harvesting.[1] By Zacchaeus's time, the word had come to refer to informers and shakedown artists of all kinds.

Zacchaeus's life changed radically on the day Jesus came to his town. Great crowds gathered around Jesus, and Zacchaeus was curious to find out who this man was. The word had gotten around about Jesus' bold teaching and his miracles and good works, and Zacchaeus wanted to see him for himself. But he had a problem. He was a short man and could not see over the crowd.

According to Luke 19:1-10, Zacchaeus solved his height deficiency by *climbing up into a sycamore tree.* (The sycamore tree in Israel was not the famous sycamore maple that people in America are used to, but rather the type of fig tree that had given fig-shakers their name.) As Jesus walked by the place where Zacchaeus was hiding, he did something unpredictable. He looked up into the tree and called Zacchaeus by name. "Zacchaeus, hurry and come down, for I must stay at your house today" (verse 5).

What an amazing thing! The Bible doesn't say how Jesus knew Zacchaeus's name, but the strange thing is not that he knew it, but rather that he *used* it. If Jesus had looked up in the tree and said, "Sycophant, come down," everyone in the crowd would have burst out into raucous laughter. "Finally, the fig-shaker got shaken down himself!" Jesus could have enjoyed great popularity by such a joke at Zacchaeus's expense.

But what Jesus said—"Come down, Righteous Man"— shook Zacchaeus down. The shakedown artist was all shook up. Immediately, he got down out of that tree and took Jesus to his home for a meal. Through this experience with Jesus, Zacchaeus encountered God. When he met God, he finally saw himself—not only for what he had become but for what he could become. In Jesus, God had shown Zacchaeus the righteous self that God intended to make him.

After lunch with Jesus, Zacchaeus stood up and announced to all the people who had gathered around his house, "Look, Lord! Here and now I give half of my possessions to the poor, and if I have cheated anybody out of anything, I will pay back four times the amount."[2] The gospel of Luke was originally written in Greek, and the word "cheated" is a translation of the Greek word *sycophanteo*, which is the same word (in verb form) as *sycophantes*. Zacchaeus recognized that he was a sycophant, but on the day he found God through Jesus, he discovered his God-given deep dream. He would live up to the promise of his name, no longer hated by those around him. He would no longer be known for stealing and informing and false dealing; instead, he would be known as a man who made things right. He would become a generous man, a credit to society. As he committed himself to that God-given dream, he changed his life and began to fulfill his true self—Zacchaeus the Righteous Man.

Like Zacchaeus, we will never fully know ourselves and fulfill the dream God desires to give us until we have a personal encounter with God. Like Zacchaeus, many people live a form of life that is not worthy of their true potential. At times people will say, "I don't know why I did that. I'm not feeling myself today." But many people live their whole lives that way. They never have a sense of who they really are. They never find themselves, because they haven't seen their true selves in God.

No one should make the mistake of thinking that I am saying human beings are gods. That is not true. As Father Cavanaugh says in the sports movie *Rudy*, "In thirty-five years of religious study, I have only come up with two hard, incontrovertible facts: There is a God, and I'm not him."[3] There is a big difference between our all-powerful, all-knowing, all-present Creator and us. Still, despite the differences between God and humanity, our true nature is like God. The Bible teaches that when humanity was created, God made us — both male and female — in God's image and likeness.[4]

Like Zacchaeus, our true selves are righteous, holy, and good. In high school, I had a teacher who explained to me that he was not a Christian because Christians believe people are basically bad. In contrast, he believed people were basically good. It was a real shame that he thought that way about Christians. True biblical Christianity does not believe people are basically wicked. Rather, it teaches that our truest nature is good, created in the image and likeness of God. God's likeness in us has been corrupted by sin, but it has not been destroyed. Every one of us can reconnect to that essential goodness God built into us at the Creation.

How do we become the good creatures God made us to be? We need a cleansing, renewing, transforming encounter with God. We need to be reconciled with God. When we go to God seeking that reconciliation, God will make himself known to us and we will be changed. Like Zacchaeus, we will be conformed to the image of God.

So how do we achieve such a meeting with God? We do it by finding out who Jesus Christ is. When we examine the life of Jesus Christ, we find the one person who was consistently like God. Jesus did good and not evil every day of his life.[5] He healed the sick[6] and showed mercy to the guilty.[7] He taught the wisdom of God in everything he said and did.[8] His life was never tainted by committing sins,[9] and his relationship with God was unbroken.[10] His entire life was dedicated to serving God and loving his neighbor.

In the end, wicked men, both Gentiles and Jews, who were threatened by Jesus' perfection, took his life away.[11] They judged him falsely, beat him without mercy, and nailed him to a cross. On that cross, the sin of every human being who ever lived was visited on the person of Jesus.[12] He was perfect innocence punished for the totality of wickedness.[13] In taking our sins on himself, Jesus paid a terrible price for what we had broken: fellowship with God. But it is not just our sins Jesus bore. He also took our sorrows on himself.[14] Every disappointment, every injustice, every tragedy or pain we have ever suffered, he shared with us. In bearing our sins, he swept away every reason for God to reject us. In bearing our sorrows, he swept away every reason for us to reject God.

Can you see your own suffering in Jesus? Can you see every punishment you ever deserved laid upon Jesus in the punishment he took on himself? If you can see your sin on him, you can know that God does not want to punish you. If you can see your sorrows in him, you can know that he loved you more than anyone ever has. If you can see yourself in him, you can become the person God made you to be: a person like Jesus.

Somehow, in a way only God can fully understand, Jesus' death restores our fellowship with God. When we look to him and see him crucified for our sins and our sorrows, when we see his death and suffering as our own, we are changed. We can no longer stand to be separated from God. We realize that fellowship with God is exactly the thing we want most. So we go to God, asking him to receive us, asking him to cleanse us and change us and be with us. Because that is the one thing God truly wants from us, he will always answer our prayer.

That's when we can begin to walk in friendship with God. Just as Jesus went to Zacchaeus's house and had dinner with him, Jesus offers to do the same for us. In Revelation 3:20 he says, "Here I am! I stand at the door and knock. If anyone hears my voice and opens the door, I will come in and eat with him, and he with me" (NIV). This fellowship with Jesus is the most precious thing a human being can know, and it will change you.

For me, the most compelling testimony of God's power to change people and give them a deep dream is the story of my own father, James Jackson Castleberry. My father died in 2004 at the age of sixty-nine, and I am writing this story on September 15, his birthday. When I preached at his funeral, I had the privilege of publicly telling the story of how my dad lived his life.

Jack Castleberry was born with a congenital heart defect. The doctors told his parents he would not live a long life, and no one ever expected him to amount to much. He was a sickly child — too small and weak to excel in the sports he loved. His tenant-farming family was very poor and he had no social standing, but little Jack decided at some point in his childhood that he would make the most of his life. Like with many people, the seeds of his deep dream began to sprout early in his life. But those sprouts were exceedingly tender, and the course of his life often threatened to crush them.

Jack was too skinny to play football when he got to high school, so he became the team manager. Then a great thing happened in his life: His brother Jean came back from the navy on leave and bought a big Pontiac convertible. When Jean's leave ended and he went back to his ship, he left the car in Jack's care. Now vested with the management of the football team and a nice new convertible, Jack became the official transporter and best friend of the cheerleading squad. Although he knew his life would be short, he no longer saw any reason for it to be boring!

Jack became a big man on campus. He gained confidence and hope. After getting a summer job in the local paper mill, he decided he would make a career in manufacturing. In his senior year, his high school classmates named him "Most Likely to Succeed." His motto, published in the school yearbook, was "Life is what you make it." Even if he was dealt a bad heart and a short life, he came to believe that everyone deserved a chance and that anyone could make life worth living if he or she worked hard enough at it.

Jack had become an optimistic, strong-minded, popular young man who was determined to make something out of his life. He believed he would succeed and was committed to working hard to achieve something. After graduation, Jack got a permanent job in the paper mill, sweeping the floors for seventy-five cents an hour. Even though his grades were not good enough for him to see himself as "college material," he was smart and capable, and he believed he would become *somebody*.

Within a few years, Jack's life began to deteriorate. He was smoking cigarettes, drinking alcohol, and seeking all the pleasures his fat salary could buy his skinny self. He gradually began to lose sight of his dream to make the most of himself and settled into a self-destructive pattern that threatened to ruin his life.

During that period of Jack's life, some friends invited him to go to church. He did not want to go but finally went to get them off his back. He arrived late at the church service, but not too late. He got there in time to hear the evangelist speak about Jesus, and as the man spoke, Jack came face-to-face with God. As soon as the opportunity to accept Christ as his Savior was offered, Jack got up and literally ran to the front of the church. That night, his whole life changed. For the rest of his life, he would never smoke another cigarette or drink alcohol. I never heard a vulgar word come out of his mouth. He was completely and utterly changed. His self-destructive ways came to an end, and his dream of a fulfilling life was reborn and transformed. Rather than making the most of life for himself, he began to dream of serving God to the full.

Jack Castleberry spent the rest of his life pursuing that dream. He worked hard at the paper mill and began to rise in the ranks. After achieving the highest rank possible for members of the labor union, he was offered a foreman's position with another company. All along the way, he was a witness of God's love to the men and women who worked with him. As I grew up and joined him for summer work in the paper mill, I saw and heard the respect and admiration other workers had for my dad.

Serving God at work was never enough. Jack served as a deacon and Sunday school teacher at church. He began going to prisons to minister to men who were deprived of their physical liberty. He became president of the Full Gospel Business Men's Fellowship. He got ministerial credentials and later started a small, multiracial church among very poor people, serving as its pastor along with his wife, Carolyn.

By the time Jack retired from the paper mill, he was manager of the pulp mill and wood yard. He had risen to the highest rank he could, and he earned a professional-class salary. Now his greatest desire was to serve God and his neighbors full-time in his retirement.

Along with Carolyn, Jack got involved in politics and eventually accompanied her as a delegate to their party's national convention. I still have the photo that came out in the *Washington Post* of my father and stepmother having fun at the convention in San Diego. He served as party vice chairman in his county and worked hard to promote a better society in America. He became a friend to the powerful and the poor. All this time, he also served as a volunteer chaplain at the local hospital, where he spent many hours comforting the sick and dying.

In the last year of his life, Jack began to suffer strange pains all over his body. Though he usually went to the hospital as a chaplain, he eventually had to walk in as a patient. He never left the hospital again. A month later he died and went on to the presence of God.

While he was in the hospital, I asked my father a series of questions about his life, including, "What was the most fun you ever had?" Many men might have answered that it was hauling the cheerleaders to the football games and partying with them afterward. Others would have focused on sporting events and vacations and travel. Others might have talked about times with their children. Dad had experienced much enjoyment in all of these ways. But he answered, "The most fun I ever had was when I got saved and began to know the Lord."

That was indeed the moment that saved my dad's life and secured his deep dream. At his funeral, I was struck that extremely humble people from his church were sitting beside judges and politicians and other eminent citizens. Everyone who met Jack Castleberry was made better by knowing him, which is the mark of a godly man. Jack succeeded in his deep dream of making the most of his life for God.

Shortly after his death, a resolution was offered in the state legislature honoring my father for his contribution to the betterment of life in his state. A poor son of tenant farmers had become *somebody*. His humility in all his successes was evidenced by his constant explanation that he owed it all to God. He always said that if Jesus had not saved him, he would never have achieved anything. That is how he taught me the greatest truth I know: When you have found yourself in Christ, you are ready to discover your deepest, God-given dream.

GO DEEPER

1. Think about the person of Christ punished on the cross. Can you see yourself in him? If faith has risen up in your heart and you see the possibility of friendship with God through Jesus, please pray in your own words to restore your relationship with God.

If you would like, pray the following words. If you pray them with sincerity, they will become your words, just as if you had composed them yourself.

Dear God, I want to be your friend. I know that my mistakes and sins have kept us apart, but I also believe that Jesus has taken all the punishment I should have received. I also know he shared my sorrows to set things right between me and God. I have found my true self in Jesus, so come into my life and be with me. I need your help to become the person you made me to become. Make something noble and beautiful and good out of my life. Take over control of my life. I am ready to obey you and follow your lead. I surrender to you every dream I have ever had, so that I can fulfill your dream for me.

2. As soon as you can, tell a person whom you know to be a serious Christian about the prayer you prayed.

3. In your own words, express thanks to God for giving you your life. Thank him for giving you a destiny and a dream. Thank him for being present with you and for his promise to walk with you until your life and dreams are fulfilled.

4. Take time to write out the story of your life up to this point. If you prefer, just write down a few bullet points or phrases. Whether you just now encountered Jesus or have known him for years, try to describe how meeting Jesus is helping you discover your truest self. This testimony is one of the greatest things you can share with another person, so share it with as many people as will listen.

CHAPTER 4

EMBRACE YOUR DESTINY

Václav Havel was born in Czechoslovakia in 1936, the son of a successful businessman. Early in his youth, he began to dream of being an artist and intellectual. But after World War II, his country fell under communism and wealthy families like his found themselves opposed by the government. Despite Havel's talent and love for the arts, the government forced him to study at a technical university instead of going to an arts school.[1] When he finished his technical studies, he began obligatory service in the army, where he had his first experience in theater. Before long, he was establishing quite a reputation as a playwright, bringing both admiration and trouble as he artfully critiqued the communist government.

Within a decade, Havel's plays began to have an important role in the life of his country. In 1968 he and other thinkers succeeded in getting the government to allow more freedom of speech. For a few months, later known as the Prague Spring, hope began to rise throughout Eastern Europe and the rest of the world. People began to believe that the worst times of Soviet rule in Eastern Europe might be lifting. But that hope was crushed when the Soviet Union sent tanks and troops rolling into Prague. As spring evaporated into summer, a season of hot oppression descended on the country.

Faced with the threat of prison, Havel did not give up his convictions about freedom of expression. The government quickly silenced him by banning his subversive plays. He had to work as a manual laborer in order to survive. Still, Havel became the main leader of the Czech resistance. He stopped writing plays and started writing political letters and essays. Imprisoned three times for his defense of freedom, he never submitted to the silence that evil men tried to impose on him. As a result, his condemnation of communism became known around the world. He began to have an impact beyond his own nation.[2]

Havel played an important part in the fight against communism. Along with other world leaders such as Pope John Paul II, Margaret Thatcher, and Ronald Reagan, Havel gradually chipped away the foundation of Soviet power. When the Berlin Wall fell and communist control of Eastern European governments began disintegrating in 1989, Havel's country gained its freedom. This nonviolent overthrow of communism led by artists and thinkers became known as the Velvet Revolution. Havel's leadership was reflected in the fact that in 1989, he was elected president of a newly democratic Czechoslovakia. After the country peacefully divided into two nations, he also served as president of the Czech Republic.

It had not been Havel's dream to become a politician. His passion was the theater, and he probably would have been happy to serve simply as a playwright and artist. But opposition and oppression changed a velvet man into a man of steel. Instead of being destroyed by his enemies, he used the heat of their attacks to forge a bigger dream for himself and his country.

Havel summarized an important lesson when he said, "The real test of a man is not when he plays the role he wants for himself, but when he plays the role destiny has for him."[3] Havel's saying is important for any man or woman who would live out a dream. It is not enough simply to dream. We need to embrace the dream that fits our destiny. If we do not find it, we will spend our lives in pursuit of things that will not bring us ultimate fulfillment.

Anyone who believes in destiny believes, at some level, that there is a purpose in the world and that we each have a role in it. While some people do not want to admit it, the Lord of destiny is God. Destiny is real. Every person was designed with a purpose, because God designed each of us.

People often have a wrong idea about what destiny is. Many think of destiny and fate as being the same thing—the inevitable future that will happen to you no matter what you do. People of various religions, including some Christians, believe the future is predestined and we can do nothing to change it. The world's greatest philosophers have never been able to prove whether or not all details of the future are predetermined, and neither have scientists. The great physicist Stephen Hawking of Cambridge University has said that the issue is too complicated for us to ever figure out. Although he thinks everything is probably predetermined, he says you can't live your life that way.[4]

I don't believe everything is predetermined by God, but rather that human beings have free will and can decide a few things for themselves. But I do believe in destiny. There are things we simply cannot change. We can't change the past, including such crucial things as who our parents were. Our genetic makeup is also pretty much set, though we seem to be entering a time when it will be possible to tweak it. We cannot determine whether we begin our lives in a free society or in some kind of totalitarian state. While we can work together with others to make positive changes in the world, we are unable to determine whether we will live in times of economic boom or recession (although everyone will see both during their lifetime, usually several times). There are many things we cannot change.

At the same time, there are things we do seem to be able to change. We may not be able to decide whether or not we are bald, but we can decide whether to shave our head or wear a wig. We may be unable to make a big change in our IQ, but we can decide to study and make the most of the intelligence we have. We may not be the next candidate for supermodel, but we can decide whether to dress well and look as good as we can.

I believe God has given each of us a destiny. It is a combination of all the things in our past that affect and even determine our future, all the opportunities and challenges that will come our way over the course of our lifetime, our talents and weaknesses, our national identity and ethnic heritage, and many other things. It also includes the future God will give us if we cooperate with his plan.

That last "if" is a big one. I believe that the most important part of our destiny is the part we have some control over. Will we or will we not embrace our challenges and opportunities and make the most of them, fulfilling God's plan for our lives and enjoying the amazing satisfaction that comes from realizing God's good destiny for us? The alternative is to throw away the future that could be ours and the contributions we could make to the people around us. To the degree we choose the latter, we will waste our lives. To that same degree, we risk ending up bitter, lonely people full of regrets. We risk failure to discover and live out our deep dream.

If we do not find the dream that fits our destiny — if we do not discover what God made us to do — we will spend our lives in pursuit of things that will not bring us ultimate fulfillment. People follow unworthy dreams all the time. Some dream of an unlimited supply of drugs, others are sex addicts, money-grubbers, power freaks, or glory-seekers. Does anyone admire such people? Is there any honor in what they seek? Are such dreams worthy of human beings?

It is not enough to have a dream. Dreams that fulfill us need to correspond to who we are as beings made in the image of God. That means that no vile or ignoble or ugly thing can truly satisfy us. There is no cheap way, no easy road. There is no shortcut.

There is only one way we will ever find the dream that will truly fulfill us: by recognizing our destiny and embracing it. Cru (formerly Campus Crusade for Christ) is a ministry known around the world for producing tracts about the "Four Spiritual Laws," which tell people, "God loves you and offers a wonderful plan for your life." That is the truth. To borrow a line from the Westminster Shorter Catechism, the chief end of humanity is "to glorify God, and to enjoy him forever."[5] I believe the Scriptures make it clear that God wants everyone to achieve that very end. (Indeed, it is an "end" that never ends.) The Bible says in 2 Peter 3:9, "The Lord is . . . patient toward you, not wishing that any should perish, but that all should reach repentance." Many people accomplish great things in this world that they were destined by God to achieve, but the full realization of their destiny requires that they come to know God. Ultimately, to fulfill our highest destiny, we need to find and walk with God.

Some people may want to ask, "What about people who are born with disabilities? What is their destiny? Does God have a wonderful plan for their lives?" They might suggest that the existence of disabilities is proof that God is not good and does not love us or that God does not exist at all. My answer is that God absolutely does have a plan to bring blessing into the lives of people who are born with special challenges!

Many people have to deal with depression, bipolar disorder, schizophrenia, and other serious mental diagnoses. On a far less dramatic level, a large percentage of human beings struggle with attention deficit disorder. People who are born with mental and cognitive challenges—like everyone else—will struggle all the days of their lives. But the most shallow glance through history reveals that such people have achieved many great things. It is widely believed, for example, that Albert Einstein suffered from Asperger's syndrome, a form of autism.[6]

With some profound disabilities, a person might not have the mental capacity to conceive of such a thing as destiny or a dream. But God can use such people to affect the lives of others in a way that brings love, depth, and even joy into their lives. God sees so much more of reality than we do.

Surely struggle is a basic part of the life journey of every human being. In too many cases, people with severe challenges, like people with more ordinary challenges, will fail to live out the wonderful plan of God. But others will not fail. Those who find a relationship with God, which provides guidance and purpose in the midst of challenge, will find a great source of help.

When I was a pastor, a couple came to me asking for prayer. They wanted their Down syndrome child to be healed. If the child had been sick, I gladly would have prayed and asked God to heal him. But I counseled the parents that there was nothing wrong with their child. Their problem was not an intellectually disabled child but rather a society that fails to discern the value of such children. God can give lives of great satisfaction and worth to intellectually challenged people whose families love them and work with them to build lives of dignity.

Years ago while I was in seminary, I worked in a factory in Trenton, New Jersey. Every day after work I would get on a bus and ride back to Princeton, where I lived. One of the riders I saw every day was a mentally challenged young man. He was able to ride the bus by himself to his daily activities, which seemed to include a job. He knew several people who habitually rode the bus at that time and would exchange pleasantries with them. When it came time for him to get off the bus, he would stand up, check his back pocket to confirm his wallet was there, smile, say good-bye to the bus driver, and get off the bus. Then he would walk toward his home.

Watching his routine every day, I came to value him as an example of a truly dignified person. He was meeting his challenge every day with a great attitude and a sweet spirit. While I never got to talk to him in any depth about his life, I think he was living out his dream of being a productive person in society, making his own living, being a blessing to others, not bowing to the cruel things other children must have said to him when he was young. There was not a soul in Trenton I had greater respect for.

Where did we get the idea that struggle and challenge are somehow evidence of a defective life? Does anyone think that CEOs and other highly successful people live a life free of struggle and challenge? The problem is that our society applauds the struggle of those it considers "highly successful." But it stands back with a feeling of self-satisfied pity for those whose struggle does not produce a high income and/or social status. Even if society cannot see it, human struggles can bring fulfillment to those who face them with dignity.

One of the greatest American songwriters of the twentieth century was Hank Williams, and one of the greatest novelists was Ernest Hemingway. Unfortunately, both suffered greatly from severe depression. Hank Williams died too young, likely due to a combination of drugs and alcohol, in the back of a car on his way to a New Year's Eve show. Hemingway ended his own life with a shotgun. Both deaths were tragedies that were *not* God's plan for these precious, artistically blessed lives. But no one should misjudge their lives. Both men lived lives that turned struggle and challenge into prodigious art.

Their lives had inestimable worth. Both achieved things they dreamed about, important elements of their destinies. But I fear neither of them fulfilled the life he could have had if he had walked with God all his life. A contrasting example would be Charles Haddon Spurgeon, who suffered from crippling depression for most of his life. But he found the grace to become one of the greatest preachers in history, living his entire life for the glory of God over and against his struggle with depression.

Every person who faces special challenges in life, whether mental or physical, must find God in order to discern God's purpose for himself or herself in the midst of struggle. Not everyone can do it in a way society will consider to be "high-functioning." But no one should ever despair of finding God's purpose for his or her life, or of discovering a deep dream to pursue.

The majority of those who will read this book have ordinary struggles. The story of Václav Havel raises an important issue: People do not really know the full extent of their deep dream when they are children. While some children have a pretty clear idea of the future they want, the full vision can only be seen as we grow. Growth in seeing our destiny comes as we struggle against opposition. Rather than seeing opposition as destructive, we should accept it as a necessary element. It will help us define not only the role we want in life, but also the role destiny has assigned to us.

Go Deeper

1. If you could achieve anything you wanted, what would it be? Please do not answer this question with "fame" or "fabulous wealth" or something else that does not bring true fulfillment, even to those who achieve it. Write down something that relates to your abilities, talents, tastes, and hopes.

2. How have the circumstances of your life shaped your ability to pursue the thing you want the most?

3. Make a list of the five activities that bring you the most pleasure and satisfaction.

4. What might your future look like if you were to allow these five things to work together in some way toward a common goal?

5. Given the circumstances of your life, what is the thing you believe God would most want you to accomplish?

It is likely that your last two answers are similar. If not, ask yourself why God would give you talents and gifts for something that is not related to God's will for your life. Surely God does not think that way!

CHAPTER 5

BE WILLING TO
BE A LEADER

We often see images of the Reverend Dr. Martin Luther King Jr. giving his "I Have a Dream" speech. Many people would say there has never been a more powerful speech in all of history. That inspiring moment on the National Mall in Washington, DC, seemed to prove that dreams can change the world. But the truth is, dreams don't change the world. People who participate in dreams change the world.

Without the thousands of people who were standing on the National Mall that day, Dr. King's speech would never have happened. It was the whole civil rights movement, not just the speeches or the dream, that had such a profound impact. The secret to Dr. King's success was the people he was able to lead in pursuing his dream.

You need to understand something if you are planning to be a successful dreamer: You are going to need help! No dream can be accomplished by one person alone. We simply are not built that way. Healthy human beings live in a state of interdependence. We need each other.

If you want to fulfill your dream, you need to get people to help you accomplish it. There is a word for someone who organizes the efforts of others to achieve a vision or a dream: *leader*. The truth of the matter is that the only person who can lead the vision for your personal deep dream is YOU.

From early in his life, Dr. King knew he had a calling to serve people. He later said, "My call to the ministry . . . was not a miraculous or supernatural something, on the contrary it was an inner urge calling me to serve humanity."[1] In order to pursue that calling, he rushed through his high school training. At age fifteen, he went to Morehouse College, where he was a brilliant student. His thinking became very sophisticated during college, seminary, and doctoral studies, as he was inspired by the ideas of such leaders as William Rauschenbusch, Paul Tillich, and Mahatma Gandhi.

Dr. King was only twenty-five years old in 1954 when he and his new wife, Coretta, went to pastor the Dexter Avenue Baptist Church in Montgomery, Alabama. He had no idea his work at the church would result in the civil rights movement. The young Dr. King had all the intellectual preparation he needed to engage his deep dream. But he could not have predicted the way his contact with ordinary church people would push him forward.

After so many years in an academic atmosphere, he had become very brainy. Indeed, he had distanced himself from the emotional faith he had grown up around in church. Preferring a rational approach to religion, he carefully prepared his sermon manuscripts beforehand and coolly delivered them without the passionate tones he later became famous for. He was more interested in a God of ideas than a God of personal relationship. His relationship with his people, however, changed him.

On December 5, 1955, Dr. King's approach to God changed. He was speaking at a rally of thousands of people who had gathered to support Rosa Parks after her arrest for refusing to sit at the back of the bus. At that rally, Dr. King saw "poor working people who, unlike [him], talked to God every day and lived their toilsome lives in an elevated world of Spirit."[2] Dr. King had run smack into the presence of God among a suffering people. He was overwhelmed. Instead of preaching his suave, prepared sermon that night, he began to speak out of his heart. There is a big difference between "speaking a message" and "speaking *to people*." King's speech became a combination of his own ideas, the passion of his people, and the spiritual presence of God.

That night changed Dr. King's life. From that point on, he spoke spontaneously at rallies, focused on the people as much as on his message. He began to speak not only "to" people but "for" them. His famous "I Have a Dream" speech in 1963 was unscripted. It was a textbook example of how a person's training, passion, and faith can be catapulted to the level of greatness through the process of leading other people.

Every successful person must be a leader of his or her own dream. This implies that you cannot be a successful human being unless you have a dream and work to fulfill it. If you have ever said to yourself, *I'm not a leader*, that was not very good thinking. It certainly was not realistic thinking. It was false humility, a lack of self-esteem, or a fundamental misunderstanding of the nature of leadership and human interaction. The truth is, in order to achieve your deep dream and fulfill your destiny, there is no way around being a leader.

Because I wrote in the last chapter about the dreams of people with mental disabilities, some may ask how such people can exercise leadership. Even in the case of profound mental challenges, people can exercise a form of primal leadership that may not be as verbally eloquent as we often expect leadership to be. Down syndrome kids, for example, are known to be very affectionate. They often succeed in leading through example as they love in their homes. Their dream may be as simple as wanting to live in an environment of hugs and acceptance, and without articulating that dream, they lead by loving first. Leading by example is in no way inferior to leading with words, and it is infinitely superior to leadership that is all words, no action.

In some cases, leadership may be even more subtle and unintentional. Little Evelyn Mandi was born with triploidy, a chromosomal defect that usually results in death within just a few hours or days of birth. When Evelyn sent me a Facebook invitation through her loving parental "secretaries," I congratulated her for her leadership. Because of her life, people were praying, a community became more aware of its love for her parents, and many of us were longing more for heaven. It was, I told her, an amazing achievement for one so young. As she died a few hours later, I reflected on the priceless quality of her primal leadership.

No matter what a person's level of ability may be, it is impossible to have a truly satisfying life in any area of work—whether in the market or in the home or in any other workplace—without exercising the art of leadership. That makes understanding leadership an important task. Fortunately, there is a mountain of good information available for people who want to learn more about leadership. But you cannot avoid the responsibility of being a leader if you want to accomplish your deep dream.

Your question should be, "How does a person get help to accomplish a dream?" Let's look at Joseph of Egypt again and see what we can learn from his example. His first attempts to recruit helpers for his dream of honor and family leadership were a disaster. His childish method was to tell his parents and siblings that he dreamed they were all going to bow down and honor him. By spilling the beans about his dream too early to the wrong people, Joseph created resentment among his brothers and shock in his parents—not a good way to go.

Say your dream includes rising to senior management in your company (and surely it is a little broader than that!). It might not be a good strategy to go around to all your co-workers and bosses and let them know that their mission, should they decide to accept it, is to vault you to a position of wealth and power. They are not likely to sign on to that mission. So how do people get the influence needed to lead their deep dreams?

In 1957, two brilliant sociologists, John French and Bertram Raven, published an article called "The Bases of Social Power." By social power, they meant what is often called either authority or influence over other people. In their study, they identified five sources of social influence.

One source is called ***reward power***. That's the ability to reward people for doing what you want them to do. A second source is the opposite: ***coercive power***, or the power to punish people for *not* doing what you want them to do. A third source is ***expert power***. You have expert power when people recognize you as having special training or knowledge in a particular area. We often refer to someone who has special expertise in a subject as an *authority* in that field. When people believe you know more than they do about something, they will often submit to your judgment. ***Legitimate power*** is the most obvious source of power. It comes from position. When you have been elected or appointed to a position of authority through a process people see as legitimate, they will obey you or yield to your influence because of your position.

The problem with these kinds of power is that they do not win friends for you. As a matter of fact, they alienate people. Even reward power can create resentment in people upon whom it is exercised. People don't really want to do something they would not do if no one was paying or otherwise rewarding them.

Because these kinds of power alienate people from you, they are not much good for attracting people to the cause of helping you achieve your dreams. For that, you will need the fifth source of power that French and Raven discovered. It is called *referent power*. Referent power is the power that comes from people identifying with you. When people like you—when they want to *be* like you—they will let you influence them. Some people seem to get what amounts to a free pass in this area. They have what is called *charisma*. They are so comfortable with themselves, so much at ease in their own skin, that other people like to be around them. We are just naturally drawn to such people.

Often we assume that charisma is an inborn quality. It seems like some people are just born leaders. At least that's the way the folk wisdom goes. But it isn't true. Nobody gets a free pass in life. The truth is that people who do not have charisma today can acquire charisma tomorrow. How? How can we gain the charisma that will bring us referent authority and make other people want to help us achieve our dreams? Read carefully here, because what is coming next is one of the most important things in this book: When you know yourself and learn to love yourself, you can learn to love other people. When your love for yourself flows out of an understanding that you are a child of God, who loves you and has appointed you to a wonderful destiny, you find an unshakable basis from which to love other people. (Of course, there is no bad basis for loving people, and there is no question that there are atheists who love other people too. But it is easier, and indeed different, when you have understood God's love for you.)

The same way God loves you, he loves other people. When we learn to love ourselves because God loves us, we can love other people because God loves them. From that rich knowledge, we can learn to serve other people to the full.

In the Bible, one of God's commands to the Israelites was to love God with all of their heart, soul, and strength.[3] Jesus declared this the greatest of all the commandments. He went on to say that the second most important commandment was to love your neighbor as you love yourself.[4] All these things are intimately connected.

When we learn to love God, we can learn to love ourselves. When we learn to love ourselves, we can begin to love other people. When we love other people, love will break out in service, and when we serve other people, some of them will find the desire to serve us. When that happens, we have acquired referent power.

There's a tired old saying that "people don't care how much you know until they know how much you care." When people see that you care about them and are willing to serve them, they are more likely to be drawn to you and to want to help you. When that happens, you have become the leader of the project that will result in the fulfillment of your dreams.

There is a real scarcity of leadership in the world. More than anything else, people need leadership in order to live fulfilling lives. They need leaders who will inspire them and give them something to live for. The main thing leaders do is provide a vision or dream for the people following them. James MacGregor Burns calls these leaders transformational leaders and points out that by providing moral inspiration (what I am calling a dream or vision) to other people, they create new leaders in their train.[5]

Many people are not confident enough to come up with an original dream of their own which will bring fulfillment to their lives. So, they stand around living those lives of quiet desperation we talked about at the beginning of this book. One of the ways God directs such people is by putting leaders in their path who can help them realize their own destinies and commit themselves to fulfilling their own deep dreams.

Martin Luther King Jr. was such a leader. Many people living in Montgomery, Alabama, and throughout the United States in the 1950s were living in quiet desperation until he came along and began to talk to them about a better future. They needed a dream to wake them up from the nightmare they were living. Dr. King was able to help people wake up to a dream of justice and equality. As people began to believe in the dream, a movement began.

Change never happens in any society until someone comes along and articulates a vision for change. In individual lives, change never happens until a person has a dream or vision for change and begins to believe in it and act on it. The main job leaders perform is articulating a dream. When people who do not have a dream begin to participate in the dream of a leader, they gain a purpose in life. They begin to act to make a difference. They start participating in something bigger than they are. When that happens, people gain a precious human characteristic: dignity. They become leaders of their own dreams. Just as apple trees bear apple seeds that do not become pear trees, everything reproduces what it is. True leaders reproduce leaders.

Let's apply this theory to your personal life. Your dream may start out as a dream of personal glory. For example, you could dream of being the world's greatest golfer, recognized by everyone and going down in history as the best player who ever picked up a putter. You could dream of universal acclaim. But if dreams stay on that level, they are not big enough to be fulfilling. Even a small dream that is worthy of dreaming involves the cultivation of good personal character and the blessing of other people in some way. If you merely follow a dream, you can dream selfishly and settle for too little. What good would it do to be the world's best golfer if you fail to become a good man or woman? Jesus put it even more pointedly: "What does it profit a man [or woman] to gain the whole world and forfeit his [or her] soul?"[6]

Perhaps your dream is that you will be able to raise a happy family. To succeed, you will need to involve other people in accomplishing your dream. You will need to lead your family by articulating a dream and mobilizing every family member to realize it. Without your spouse, father, mother, aunts, uncles, sons, daughters, and others, there is no family to be happy. Not every family will have all these elements intact, but that does not mean those who remain cannot be happy if a happiness leader emerges. One of the things that makes "having a happy family" a noble dream is that you cannot do it by yourself. It is a dream that requires you to lead other people.

All dreams that are big enough to fulfill a human being are like that. They require you to involve other people in something bigger than they are. They require a vision of an alternative future so much better than the present that it will inspire you and other people to make sacrifices to achieve it. They require the development of good personal character. They require us to rise to a nobler level of life.

I need to make clear one more point about leadership: You do not have to be the boss to be a leader. No matter what your position in an organization, you can be a leader. You may be a recently hired floor sweeper or the president of the United States of America—it doesn't matter. Leadership is not about having all authority. God is the only one who has that level of authority. But leadership is about exercising influence on the people around you. In order to fulfill your dreams, you must be willing to use the influence you have to get other people to participate in your vision.

GO DEEPER

1. Who are the three visionary leaders you most admire? Go ahead and write down their names and the thing you admire the most about their vision:

Visionary Leaders	What You Admire About Their Vision

How have you become involved (or how could you become involved) in making at least one of their visions a reality? How does the vision they are working for relate to your own dreams?

2. Who are the people you would most like to serve? Be sure to answer this question not only on the level of specific people you know, but also in terms of groups of people — orphans or corporate CEOs or drug addicts or college students or some other social group you would like to dedicate a part or all of your life to serving.

3. In order to serve that group of people, what skills do you need to acquire or hone? What status do you need to attain in order to gain credibility with them? What tools do you need to bring to the work you have in mind?

4. Who do you admire that is serving that group now? Who is serving that group poorly in your estimation? What lessons of leadership can you learn from observing both of those people or groups of people? How could you see yourself working under someone else's leadership to develop the service you wish to offer?

5. Who would you need to get to know to help you achieve your desire to serve? How would they be helpful to you in achieving your goals, and reciprocally, how can serving you help them achieve their goals?

CHAPTER 6

BE WILLING TO SERVE OTHERS

A great story of public service comes from the life of Robert H. H. Hugman, the architect who envisioned, designed, and built the famous River Walk in San Antonio, Texas. His vision brought him fulfillment in his professional life, but also resulted in big benefits for the people of San Antonio. The Old World atmosphere of gondolas, hotels, restaurants, shops, and other attractions along the River Walk has attracted millions of tourists. Honeymooners and other romantics have embraced each other with deeper love because Hugman had the foresight, imagination, and skill to turn angry, out-of-control floodwaters into a lazy river of love boats.

Though many San Antonio residents and visitors probably cannot identify Hugman as their benefactor, a small testament to Hugman's tenacity can be found on a bronze plaque almost hidden on a building along the River Walk, or *Paseo del Rio* as it is known in Spanish:

> Robert H. H. Hugman, architect, revered for his role in development of the River Walk, 1939–1941, opened his office at river level in this circular space in early 1941. He remarked at the time,

"I opened my office at river level. When I did this, people said, in essence: 'I knew you were a dreamer, but now I know you are also a fool. You'll be drowned like a rat in your own hole.'"

In 1929, this visionary architect presented a master plan to the city of San Antonio for development of the Downtown River Bend. Hugman's plan proposed a balance between commercial and park-like qualities while maintaining the river's natural character and preserving Old World architecture.

Hugman was convinced that the ideal future of the Paseo del Rio rested in preserving the historic character peculiarly San Antonio's own; that the flavor of our Spanish, Mexican, and South-west traditions must be emphasized in all future development; that our "little river" should be treated as a stage setting on which people are transported to the unusual; that all future architectural growth avoid modern styles; and further, that the river's tempo must be jealously guarded, remaining slow and lazy, in complete contrast with the hustle and bustle of street-level modern city life. . . .

Robert H. H. Hugman is rightly deemed "Father of the River Walk."[1]

Many of the leaders of San Antonio fought against Hugman's dream, and it took years for him to accomplish it. But he persisted despite the naysayers.

Hugman started by putting his office right alongside the river, braving the floods that so often had lashed the city. He then worked to accomplish the engineering that would tame the river and attract others to the setting. In the end, he earned a place of memory and honor for giving his city a mighty push along its road from being a lonely Mexican outpost to becoming one of the most truly American cities in the United States. San Antonio now embodies the American dream, from its famous Alamo to its River Walk to its popular NBA basketball team, the Spurs.

Your deep dream may in fact be far smaller than the dreams of such people as Hugman. It may be as simple as being a person of integrity and honor, becoming a lifelong learner, having a happy marriage, raising healthy and honorable children, or serving your local community. In absolute terms, such dreams are just as important as any others. What good would the San Antonio River Walk be without love and relationships and happy people and their families and friends?

Simply put, if you want people to serve you in achieving your dreams, you have to be willing to serve them. Hugman could never have achieved his dream of building the River Walk without first choosing to serve the people of San Antonio. As he is quoted on the plaque at the River Walk, "Paseo del Rio's success will always lie in the unique aesthetic and romantic appeal experienced by people who visit and wish to share it with others."

Notice that Hugman does not say the success of the project would *depend on* its effect on people, but rather that the success would *lie in* its effect on people. It was the positive effect of the project on people's lives that made the dream worth striving for from the start. It wasn't just a selfish moneymaking scheme or even "art for art's sake." It was a project carried out to make people's lives better. I love the way Hugman envisioned that the enjoyment experienced by people would make them "wish to share it with others." Not only did Hugman want to serve people by building the River Walk, but he also wanted to turn them into servants of others.

The principle of servant leadership became an important part of business thinking when Robert Greenleaf wrote his classic book *Servant Leadership* in 1970. It is the basis for most current thinking about customer service. Serving people well builds a positive relationship with them, which not only makes them happy but also creates a sense of gratitude to the one doing the serving.

When we learn to love ourselves, we will love other people. When we love them, we will serve them in love. When people receive that kind of service, they won't forget it. Most people are self-centered and insecure during times of personal crisis. But later, after the crisis is over and the time is right, these same people will remember those who have served them well.

Now, be careful! People are not stupid, and they can see through those who are serving them in order to build up a favor account they plan to bank on later. Our reason for serving people has to be a sincere appreciation of them and a desire to help them.

The Second Great Commandment, one of the most basic teachings of Christianity, simply states, "You shall love your neighbor as yourself."[2] Implicit in this idea is the notion that you have to love yourself before you can love someone else, and that loving your neighbor implies serving their needs. True love is always more than just an emotional feeling. It is a feeling that results in kind actions and service.

While none of us should be selfish, we should not abandon the fulfillment of our own dreams and dedicate ourselves only to fulfilling other people's needs. That wouldn't take "loving yourself" seriously enough. Sometimes we serve the dreams of others in ways that only benefit them. At other times, we serve people in ways that not only serve their dreams, but directly benefit ours as well.

My friend Jackie Nelson set the standard for serving others. She was the owner of a large, successful business and was living the high life, searching for things that would make her life more exciting. As she sought, she found Jesus, and her life changed radically. "When I met Jesus, I started looking at life from the top down," she told me. "I realized that before that, I had been looking at life from the bottom up."

Jackie and her husband, Henry, bought a quaint, two-hundred-year-old mansion in the beautiful rolling hills of western New Jersey. The house was surrounded by a small farm and had a charming pond for the wild geese and ducks that always seem to fly through the Garden State. Knowing she would need a housekeeper, she sought help from the Acme Employment Agency in Brooklyn. (I know it sounds like something out of a *Road Runner* cartoon, but it's true.)

Acme sent an old Irish immigrant named Eileen, who was, frankly, a very odd person with serious health problems. Eileen had come from Ireland thirty-five years earlier to take care of a sick distant relative, but by the time she arrived, the woman had gotten better and didn't need Eileen. Eileen went to work as a housekeeper, and over the years, she became increasingly separated from her family and other people. One of her employers even tried to have her committed to an asylum. While she wasn't exactly homeless, she had never really found a home in America.

Doubled over with scoliosis, Eileen could hardly do any serious housework, but Jackie's heart went out to her immediately, and she decided to take her in and help her. Who hires a servant in order to serve them? But that was Jackie's nature. She offered Eileen a job, and Eileen moved from New York to New Jersey. Jackie's family became Eileen's family, and Jackie's home became her home.

Unfortunately, things started going wrong for Jackie. A dishonest accountant was embezzling from her business, and

before long, she lost the business. Jackie turned her attention to
serving God as principal of a Christian school, but as the full
impact of her financial losses set in, she was unable to keep up
the mortgage on her home. She tried everything she knew to
save the house, but the day finally came when she was facing
foreclosure.

As Jackie sat at the table in her kitchen looking at her unpaid
mortgage, she quietly wept over the losses she had suffered—
first the business, and now her home. Eileen saw her crying and
asked, "Miss Jackie, what's the matter?"

"We're going to lose the house unless I can pay $117,000,"
said Jackie.

Eileen left the room, returning shortly with a packet of old-
fashioned passbooks, little booklets that banks used to give
depositors to track their balance before the days of computers
and automatic tellers. As Jackie looked at the passbooks, she was
shocked to see that the balance of the books equaled $117,000.

"Eileen, can you lend me this money?"

"Sure, Miss Jackie. We can't lose our house."

"Eileen, I can't pay this money back. Can you give it to me?"

"Sure, Miss Jackie. We can't lose our house."

The accounts had been so long unattended that they had
been sent to the State Banking Commission in Albany as aban-
doned accounts. The banks had lost track of Eileen and probably thought she was dead. It turned out that many years of
interest had been lost due to inattention. Jackie and Eileen had
to track down and recover the accounts at each bank to get the
money, but they recouped the funds and saved the house,
paying off the mortgage all at once.

Jackie had intended to serve Eileen by giving her the home
she dreamed of. But her service to Eileen's dream wound up

serving her own dreams. Eileen lived in that home with Jackie and her family for the rest of her life. Jackie told me,

> No matter how feeble Eileen got later, we never sent her off to a nursing home. We had help for her forty hours a week, and the doctor, an Irishman named Moonie, used to come to the house. I insisted on having her sheets changed every day, and she used to brag about never having a bedsore at my house. The folks from hospice would come to take her away, but she'd refuse to go and would always pull through. Our family used to sing hymns to her around her bed and pray for her, and she'd get better. At the end, she went to the hospital to die. She didn't want heroic lifesaving measures, but she didn't want to starve to death like so many Irish had in years before. All she wanted was a feeding tube. The doctors wanted to disconnect it, but we never let them. We made sure she was housed and fed for the rest of her life.

Yes, Jackie set the standard for serving others, and in the process, she received help and great blessing from an unexpected source. Paying off the mortgage was an elegant combination of Jackie's dream and Eileen's dream.

In my life I have found it good to participate in some dreams that are "theirs," some dreams that are "ours," and some dreams that are "mine." I have done some things in my career that focused only on helping other people achieve their dreams. Perhaps the only benefit I got from doing so was the salary I was paid, but there is nothing wrong with being paid for service. Usually there were other indirect benefits. Sometimes serving others teaches us skills we did not expect to need. Occasionally it gives us opportunities to meet people who will turn out to be key helpers in our future. Helping others with their dreams can also give us a sense of satisfaction in doing something simply because it is a good thing to do. In whatever case, there is a lot of dignity involved in serving someone else without expectation of reward for doing it.

Sometimes, I have participated in visions or projects that were "ours" and shared more or less equally with other people in the benefits of our work. My greatest experience of an "our" dream has been joining my wife, Kathleen, in raising three daughters. Such a project takes real sacrifices, but in retrospect the satisfactions we have experienced along the way make those sacrifices seem like pure pleasure. It is a great thing to partici- pate in something that blesses everyone involved. A sense of partnership and togetherness is part of the reward we get from such projects.

Finally, I have sometimes done things that were almost totally for my own benefit. An example would be studying for my doctorate — one of the goals I needed to achieve in order to fulfill my deep dream. While my family got a side benefit from my getting a doctorate, most of the benefit came to me. I'm glad my wife was willing to take on my dream as an "our" dream and my professors served me in a "his" dream.

Undoubtedly, you can think of several activities you are engaged in that fit each of these three categories. When we live a life of service to others, we love others. If we keep our own dream intact as we serve others, then we love others just as we love ourselves. That is how we achieve our dreams by serving others.

GO DEEPER

1. Make a list of things you do to fill the following three catego- ries of service.

Their Dream	Our Dream	My Dream

2. If you have placed more items in one column than another, consider what you may be doing wrong. Are you acting selfishly, working only for yourself? Are you "hating" yourself by only serving the dreams of others? Is there anything in the "our" column in which you do not share equally in the benefits? That is, are you overestimating the concept of "we"? If so, move some of those items to the other columns. Keep in mind that sometimes the "I" dream has to wait for the other kinds.

3. What changes do you need to make in your life to make sure you are participating in all three kinds of dreams?

CHAPTER 7

LIVE A LIFE OF INTEGRITY

Nobody likes a hypocrite—someone who pretends to be something he or she is not. Everyone admires a person of integrity. Integrity begins with knowing who you are and what you believe in. But it goes a step beyond that. Not only do you know what you believe in, but you also act consistently in accordance with those beliefs. You are willing to stand up and pay a price for what you believe in. That's the essence of integrity.

Ironically, one of the greatest people of integrity in the twentieth century sat down for what she believed in. In December 1955, Rosa Parks was a forty-two-year-old seamstress in Montgomery, Alabama, riding the bus home after work. She was tired from her day's work, but she was even more tired of suffering the indignity of having to stand on the bus while white men sat. "Our mistreatment was just not right, and I was tired of it," she later wrote. "I kept thinking about my mother and my grandparents, and how strong they were. I knew there was a possibility of being mistreated, but an opportunity was being given to me to do what I had asked of others."[1] So she sat down for what she knew to be true.

People who did not grow up in the South in the mid-twentieth century may not know that it was considered extremely bad manners for a man to keep his seat anywhere if a woman was standing. But the attitude of white men toward black women was different. They were treated like they were not really people. The law required them to give up their seats to any white man. Rosa Parks had come to the point where integrity demanded she challenge that law and others that were used to mistreat her people.

Notice an important thing in what she wrote: "An opportunity was being given to me to do what I had asked of others." She realized her integrity was at stake. In her work with the NAACP, she had been involved in teaching other African-Americans to stand up for their dignity. By obeying an unfair law, she would be denying the truth of what she had taught others. So she refused to give up her seat and ran the risk of being punished by the law.

Rosa was arrested and put on trial. It was not the first time she had stood up against injustice. Several times before, she had been thrown off buses by the drivers. But this time the full weight of the law came down on her. The African-American community rallied around her and refused to cooperate with the unjust laws. They boycotted the buses in Montgomery for 381 days until finally the United States Supreme Court ruled in November 1956 that racial discrimination in transportation was unconstitutional. Rosa had won an important battle for herself and her race — that is, the human race. Even her enemies would come to benefit from her victory.

In the years to come, thousands of African-Americans would make a stand by sitting down for their rights. They staged the famous lunch counter sit-ins, in which they would go into restaurants that excluded blacks and just sit down. They would refuse to move, so they were usually dragged out by the police. In that way they got the attention of the nation, and after a few years, they had won important legal ground in the struggle for full civil rights for all Americans.

Rosa Parks knew who she was: a child of God, just like everyone else. She was a human being with as much right to fair treatment as anyone else. She worked, contributed to her community, paid her taxes, and deserved the same honor as every other citizen. So, she refused to act in ways that denied that truth. And she was willing to pay the price to defend what she knew to be true. As she reached that point, her deep dream became defined: She would dedicate herself to being a person of integrity and dignity, struggling against oppression for the liberation of people — a dream she would never stop living for. Because of her example, African-Americans made a great leap forward in achieving justice in America.

So, dreamer friend, get on with the job of cultivating integrity. Cutting corners, violating ethics, sexual promiscuity, shady dealing, even petty selfishness — these things will ruin your trustworthiness among others, and ultimately, your faith in yourself. They will undercut you at every turn and reduce your dreams to mere fantasies, or even worse, tear down everything you manage to build toward your dreams. Albert Einstein once said, "Try not to become a man of success, but rather a man of value." To become a person of integrity, this principle is crucial. You may achieve a lot of goals without integrity, but you will never fulfill your God-given deep dream.

Do you know what a Pyrrhic victory is? A Pyrrhic victory is one that costs so much that it leaves the winners without resources to defend themselves any further. When people achieve a dream through actions that have no integrity, they only achieve a Pyrrhic victory. Surrendering their integrity may bring them an immediate win, but it leaves them morally depleted and defenseless. The very next attack will defeat them.

I remember a sad story from the 1988 Olympics in Seoul, Korea. Canadian athlete Ben Johnson ran 100 meters in 9.79 seconds, making him the fastest man in history. But a few days later Olympic officials took back his gold medal because he had flunked a drug test. All the glory he had dreamed of was reduced to shame in a matter of moments. The thrill of victory went up in flames. It turned into something even worse than the agony of defeat: the hot ashes of shame.

Shame is not a politically correct concept in America today. Someone has said that in today's society, honor has been reduced to celebrity, and shame has been done away with altogether. This interesting observation explains a lot of things about our society. But it isn't totally true. It may be that shame as a social reality has gone away in America, but it has not gone away as a spiritual reality. People who act against what they know to be right will never know the sweet sleep of the righteous.

Even if no one else judges you (good luck to you on that!), you will judge yourself. That takes us back to the topic of hypocrisy. Do you know what a hypocrite is? It is someone who does not judge himself or herself enough. We all know what it is to be hypercritical. That's when you are overly critical, when you judge too harshly. Hypocritical is when you judge yourself too lightly, when you are undercritical with yourself.

People who find true fulfillment of their dreams are neither hypercritical nor hypocritical toward themselves. They judge themselves accurately and hold themselves accountable to their own principles. When you know God, you can know yourself.

When you know yourself, you have an adequate basis for judging yourself. When you judge yourself rightly and hold yourself accountable to what you know is right, you have integrity. When you judge yourself correctly, people will feel less need to judge you. And even if people judge you wrongly, you will know the truth, and ultimately, it will set you free.

The old television show *Star Trek* used to proclaim in its opening segment that outer space was the "final frontier." While *Star Trek* was a great show, outer space is *not* the final frontier. Rather, it has become almost cliché to say that the real final frontier is located in *inner space*. But to me, the true final frontier is the enjoyment of personal integrity in our senior years and retirement. (I suppose one might consider the afterlife to be the final, final frontier, but that's not what we're talking about here.)

The brilliant psychologist Erik Erikson developed a theory of human growth stages that neatly explains why integrity in the senior years is the final frontier. Erikson explained that in the course of their lives, human beings confront a series of dilemmas. They are worth explaining a little bit here.

The Basic Conflicts of the Stages of Human Development[2] (Erik Erikson)	
Birth to 12 to 18 months	Trust vs. Mistrust
18 months to 3 years	Autonomy vs. Shame/Doubt
3 to 6 years	Initiative vs. Guilt
6 to 12 years	Industry vs. Inferiority
12 to 18 years	Identity vs. Role Confusion
18 to 40 years	Intimacy vs. Isolation
40 to 65 years	Generativity vs. Stagnation
65 to death	Integrity vs. Despair

Erikson calls the first growth dilemma trust versus mistrust. Children have to learn to trust the people around them to take care of them if they are going to grow into successful adults. If they don't learn this early, it will come back to haunt them later. Similarly, as they grow through childhood, they must develop either autonomy (self-control) or shame. This is the stage where children learn to feed themselves, go to the bathroom by themselves, dress themselves, and establish self-control and independence. If they don't achieve this, they will live in shame.

In the next stage, children learn to take initiative. That is, they do things like going to kindergarten to start formal learning. They learn to entertain themselves, not depending on their mother or father to define how they play. They not only have a mind of their own, but they can act on it. If they do not learn to take initiative, they will live with a sense of guilt.

In later childhood, Erikson said children face a dilemma called industry versus inferiority. They start learning special skills that begin to define them as capable people. They learn to play sports or musical instruments. They get interested in nature or history or something else. They start collecting things. Most important, they learn how to work. If they do not start learning and discovering some special abilities, they will struggle with feelings of inferiority as they see other children developing skills.

As children grow into adolescence, the major task is to develop a sense of personal identity. If as children they developed trust of others, self-control, initiative, and industry, they will be secure for their age and will have a good degree of self-knowledge. Out of the things they know themselves to be and the things they have learned to like and do, they can develop a sense of identity. If teenagers or young adults do not develop a clear sense of identity and their roles in life, they will cast about, perhaps for the rest of their lives, looking for something to do. Or they will settle into an unfulfilling role that is easy. They will take the path of least resistance and grow into misery.

The next challenge is learning to develop intimate relationships with others. For some, this means finding a partner and learning to live in a successful marriage. For others, it means learning to share their lives with friends and family intimately. If we fail in this challenge, we are in for years of frustration and loneliness.

Another developmental task comes after we have established ourselves in a career and a happy marriage or other intimate relationships. There is an adjustment period in life that Erikson calls generativity versus stagnation. In our mid-thirties or later, we often find that our career has bogged down a bit. Perhaps we haven't reached the goals we set earlier in life. Maybe we have reached them but don't know what to do next. It is common for people to become depressed at this time or fall into what has become famous as the "midlife crisis." If we do not face this challenge squarely and figure out a new way to become forward-looking and optimistic, we can degenerate into personal stagnation. Often, to avoid stagnation, we need to adjust, clarify, and then reengage our dreams.

Ultimately, the reward for meeting life's developmental challenges successfully is integrity in old age. It is important to realize that integrity does not just pop up like a jack-in-the-box in the final stage of life. As people begin to get a sense of themselves and their values, they should develop a habit of living in a way consistent with those values. Imagine that, as a teenager, a person develops a love for farming and desires to be a farmer.

There are values that work well with the life of a farmer and values that do not. Discipline, physical fitness, good mathematical skills, a stable marriage, respect for nature, and many other values and skills are essential.

It turns out that being a great farmer goes a long way toward being a great man or woman. The integrity a farmer may have in the final stage of life is deeply dependent on the life of good character and solid values built over the course of a lifetime. Integrity throughout life yields integrity at the end of life. True integrity will never get plucked out at the end of life like a winning raffle ticket.

Imagine two unrelated people named Joe and Joan. As a child, Joe meets all the challenges of trust and self-control and industry that help form a clear identity. As he becomes an adult, he builds a few intimate and long-lasting relationships that bring emotional satisfaction to his life. He identifies the values he is going to live by and begins walking them out with integrity. He builds a career and pursues it to early successes. As middle age comes, he makes peace with his failures. His deep dream is clarified, restructured, and reengaged. Finally, Joe reaches retirement. Instead of dreading it, the highly successful Joe is looking forward to rest and free time. He spends the remainder of his life in peace and satisfaction. There are no laments of the kind that begin "If I had only . . ." or "Why didn't I . . . ?" Instead, memories of the past are celebrated with satisfaction. In the end, he never quits on his deep dream, because deep dreams are lifelong. They require us to stay on task until the day we die.

Joe has lived a life of integrity. He knows he did everything he could to make the most of his life. He realizes that while things were not perfect, they were good. Joe understands that his life was not a waste. He likes young people and does not resent their superior health and opportunities. He lives with a deep sense of integrity and fulfillment. When he dies, the church is full of mourners who think something like, "He's in a better place, but what are we going to do without him?" He's Joe Dreamer, living and dying with integrity.

Joan's life, on the other hand, illustrates the nightmare outcome. When Joan was a child, her parents were cold and distant, neglecting her and pushing her off on others to fulfill her needs, more or less. She never learned to trust people. As childhood progressed, she was a bed wetter and failed to gain other important elements of self-mastery in a timely way. When school came around, she lacked the drive to get busy and work hard, and therefore never really developed any outstanding skills to hang a sense of self-esteem or even self-knowledge on. As a teen, she just didn't know what she wanted to do. She later floated through a string of episodic relationships, sexual promiscuity, and failed marriages. By the age of thirty-five, she had given up all hope of a happy life. She became a complaining, self-pitying disaster of a person.

At any place in the journey, Joan could have surrendered her life to God, repented of her failures (whether passive or willful), shaken off her identity as a victim, and begun the reformation of her life. She could have begun a serious campaign to establish some integrity, but it would have taken a total turn-around of her life. She never found the energy to begin the campaign, despite the many people who offered to help. Although she was a legitimate victim, her failure to become a victor was her own fault.

As an old woman, Joan was bitter, angry, depressed, sick, and intolerant. She hated young people. She died in despair. No one mourned her passing. The few people at her funeral were too busy sorting out their own mixed feelings to pay her any real honor. Her grave is the physical reality of which her poor, miserable life was a symbol—a pit in the dirt. She's Joan Nightmare who lived and died in quiet desperation.

Obviously, these two cases are "pure" types, or "straw men," as the logicians say. Few people are as successful as Joe and, thanks to the mercy of God, few fail as totally as Joan. But everyone's life will probably look more like one than the other. Too many funerals are like Joan's funeral. Which story does your life most closely resemble? If the answer is Joan's, I encourage you to work on learning the principles in this book. Read until you know them by heart, and live them out at all costs. Remember: Only those who live with integrity get to die with integrity. While it is utterly impossible to be a fulfiller of dreams unless you establish a lifestyle of integrity, it is never too late to do so.

GO DEEPER

1. Think about your life and write down a few of the most important things that cause you to feel the following emotions. (Perhaps you will want to use a code word instead of a full explanation.)

Distrust			
Shame			
Guilt			
Inferiority			
Stagnation			
Despair			

The things you wrote down are precisely the things that are robbing you of integrity. Anything that breeds distrust, shame, guilt, inferiority, stagnation, or despair is not consistent with the truth that you are a human being created in the image of God.

2. You are going to have to stop doing things that create the feelings you listed. They are "sins" against yourself. I wish I could just tell you to stop doing these injuries to yourself. But for now, identify the things you need to stop doing or the things you need to stop allowing others to do to you. Go ahead and make a list of them now.

3. If doing this exercise has made you feel guilty, ashamed, or something else that is discouraging, whatever you do, do not stop reading. There is help ahead.

CHAPTER 8

BE HUMBLE

A lot of people mistakenly believe that humility is a lack of
self-esteem. Humility does not mean low self-image, self-
doubt, or low expectations. In fact, humility is the result of
having an accurate self-concept. It means you know what your
mission in life is and are content to accomplish it. When you
know who you are and what you are capable of doing, you will
neither suffer from a low self-image nor make others suffer from
your haughtiness and inflated pride. People who achieve true
humility are an inspiration to everyone.

Even God is attracted to humility. James 4:6 states, "God
opposes the proud, but gives grace to the humble." Jesus said,
"Everyone who exalts himself will be humbled, and he who
humbles himself will be exalted."[1] Not only did Jesus say that,
he also lived it out. He humbled himself by dying on the cross,
and God exalted him by making his name "the name that is
above every name, so that at the name of Jesus every knee should
bow, in heaven and on earth . . . and every tongue confess that
Jesus Christ is Lord, to the glory of God the Father."[2]

One of the world's most truly humble people in recent years
was the late Corazon Aquino, who was named *Time* magazine's
Person of the Year in 1986. She had recently defeated a dictator,
Ferdinand Marcos, to become president of the Philippines.

Certainly no one had expected such a thing would happen to her. The only job listed on her résumé before she became president was "housewife." If she could have had her wishes, she never would have run for political office.

Circumstances forced Mrs. Aquino into a role she had never dreamed of. In fact, in order to fulfill that role, she would have to live through a nightmare. As a child, she knew both comfort and danger. She was the daughter of a wealthy Filipino congressman, but her family suffered severe peril during the Japanese invasion of the Philippines during World War II, in which several of her cousins were massacred. In the turbulent times after the war, her father sent her and her brothers and sisters to study in the safety of the United States.[3]

After completing her studies in peace, she married Benigno Aquino and dreamed of a peaceful life at home. But Benigno was a patriot who had dedicated his life to overthrowing the Marcos regime and bringing freedom to his country. Corazon was proud of her husband, but she suffered a great deal as he was imprisoned, exiled, and then imprisoned again for his opposition to the dictator. Despite her suffering, she devoted herself to being a faithful, loving, and supportive wife, and a good mother to her children. She also became a woman of strong faith, with an uncanny trust in God.

Her hopes for a peaceful future with her husband and children were destroyed when her husband died a martyr's death in his struggle for Philippine democracy. As the political situation got worse and worse, people began to clamor for Corazon to take up her husband's cause and run for president against Marcos. She later reflected on the challenge very humbly, saying, "I know my limitations, and I don't like politics. I was only involved because of my husband."[4]

But people continued to call out for her. Her life depicted the tragedy of the Philippines, and people believed she understood their suffering and had the strength to lead them. She finally accepted the call of her people, but did it in an unassuming setting—while giving a speech titled "My Role as Wife, Mother and Single Parent" at a university sorority meeting.[5] Through a series of events that even the most cynical reporters and politicians called "miraculous," she defeated the dictator in the election. Though he tried to steal the election, his generals stood with the humble housewife and forced him to leave.

President Aquino took over an impossible situation and handled it in a way that astounded everyone. Her strength, serenity, honesty, and integrity became an example to the world. When she accepted the prestigious Fulbright Award after her term ended and she had peacefully given up power to an elected successor, she said:

> It has crossed my mind that this award might have come when I was the leader of an embattled democracy, to impress its enemies that Philippine freedom had important friends abroad. But I am happy that this award comes when I am again an ordinary person. After all, it all began with an ordinary person, placed by Providence at the head of quite ordinary people like herself. I am not a hero like Mandela [the winner of the previous year's Fulbright Award]. The best description for me might, after all, be that of my critics who said: She is just a plain housewife.[6]

Corazon Aquino knew exactly who she was. She knew her dream was to be a wife and mother. But being a mother was more than a biological fact for her. She plumbed the depths of motherhood, discovering the dignity, integrity, responsibility, and strength that true motherhood requires. So when the time came for her to step up and become the mother of a nation, she knew that, with God's help, she could do it. Her self-concept did not have to change in order for her to become her nation's leader, and she was happy to return to domestic life when she had done her duty. In response to her critics, Aquino once said, "I've reached a point in life where it's no longer necessary to try to impress. If they like me the way I am, that's good. If they don't, that's too bad."[7] A humble person, proud of who he or she is, can say that.

How many politicians in America would like to be president of the United States? Thousands of them! How many politicians get elected president? Very few. Extremely few. It would follow that being president of the United States is not an appropriate deep dream for the vast majority of people. Corazon Aquino never dreamed of being a president. Her dream was far nobler: to be a certain kind of person—a true mother—not just to work out the mere mechanics of any particular role.

As a matter of fact, being elected president is not a dream that will, by itself, bring fulfillment to a person. It is not enough to be president. A dream needs to include spiritual elements such as honor and integrity and peace of mind and love. If a person dreams of being a president with these qualities, it would be a wonderful thing to be president. But what good would it be to achieve the presidency without those spiritual qualities? It would be a hollow victory, even if you won by a huge landslide.

Ask Richard Nixon, the thirty-seventh president of the United States. He won the second term of his presidency by a huge margin, only to be forced to resign two years later because he tried to cover up petty and useless wrongdoing in his campaign. He had the talent to be president but had not developed the character to become a truly fulfilled person.

When it comes to the fulfillment of dreams, it is more important to have humility than to have an ambitious goal. If we have humility, it means we are content with being who we really are, and therefore, we make no pretense of being something we are not. Remember, our dreams have to be consistent with our nature, our character, and our abilities; otherwise, achieving them will be impossible.

I used to work as a busboy in a restaurant. I did it for three years, so I can tell you, being a busboy is not a pleasant job. We busboys used to say it was the lowest job in society. The truth is, there is dignity in any job. But as a busboy, you'd better carry that dignity inside of you, because there is little exterior evidence of dignity in the job.

One of my coworkers was a sweet young man of low intelligence. But he was a good busboy. One day he began telling me about how he was going to succeed in life. Although he had dropped out of high school, he bragged that he was going to go to college — to Harvard, no less. I felt so bad hearing him lay out his fantasy of success. He had no chance of graduating from or even attending Harvard. He would probably never attend any college. Even worse, if he could have somehow gotten into college, he would have been miserable there. It just didn't fit his identity or abilities.

The truth is that he had no such goal. He was just daydreaming out loud, trying to impress me because he knew I was going to college. We were always competing to see who could be recognized as the best busboy. Maybe he felt inferior. May God forgive me of anything I did to make him feel that way!

I've met other people who told me about impossible dreams. But living out a deep dream is not about setting overly ambitious goals. It is not necessarily about setting overly *specific* goals either. In its essence, living out a dream isn't primarily about reaching your goals. It is about fulfilling your personal destiny. It is about finding fulfillment as a human being. It is about being yourself at the highest level. It is a moral, spiritual vision.

Remember something about sleeping dreams. They often take aspects of our life and distort them, but even so, they sometimes reveal to us deep things about our psyche. The elements of the dream are not its meaning, but they point to a meaning beyond themselves. For example, if I have a dream about a lion, the meaning probably has something to do with my perpetual desire to be "king of the forest." It's unlikely that I'd be dreaming about a literal, upcoming safari to Kruger National Park in South Africa.

Dream elements—whether in sleeping dreams or deep dreams—tend to be symbolic. If the elements of the dream are taken too literally, they may distort the meaning of the dream. Similarly, goals may be included in the structure of a deep dream, but they distort that dream if they are taken too seriously. Being a dreamer is not a matter of achieving every goal, every detail of your dream. It's primarily about deeper, big-picture things.

Can I tell you something about my own life and dreams? For many years now, since my college years at least, I have known exactly what I wanted to become in life based on knowledge of my own nature:

- Because I have loved the Lord since childhood, I always wanted to walk in close relationship to God, hearing and obeying his voice.
- Because I know I am a lover of learning, I wanted to be a scholar who writes books and articles.
- Because I am a people person, I wanted to practice a

profession that lets me work with people and serve them. (As a busboy in high school, I turned down pay raises that would have taken me into the kitchen. I wanted to stay out in the dining room where I could see and interact with the people I was serving.)

- Because I come from a proud family that has always sought to be honorable (I have portraits of eight generations of my family on the wall at home!), I wanted to be an honorable person who has the respect of other people around me.
- Because my family rose out of poverty to join the middle class, it was important to me to prosper economically.
- Because I love meeting people and cultures that are different from my own, I wanted to travel and live for a significant time in other countries.
- Because I learn languages rapidly, I wanted to be multilingual.
- Because I am creative, I wanted to be a leader and do innovative things and lead others in projects that would achieve things never done before.
- Because I come from a family that spent time together and told stories and laughed and played, I wanted a happy family of my own. (One of my earliest memories was of wanting to grow up and have a child who would be as happy as I was!)
- Because I knew and shared the pain my own parents experienced in their divorce, I wanted to live my whole life in one happy marriage.

On these foundation stones of self-knowledge, I built a life of dreams. I would become a scholar and a minister. I would love my future wife with all my heart and establish a happy home with our own biological or adopted children. I would spend a season of my life living overseas as a missionary and, later, ministering around the world. I would live in a way that would bring honor on me and on my family, and I would prosper in my career, my home, and my inner life. I would love God and seek out eternal values. Those were the dreams I started adult life with, and I have been living them ever since.

When I was twenty-one years old, God spoke to me during a moment of great sadness in my life and promised me I would someday lead a university. As a result, I began to work toward one of the most ambitious dreams of my life — to become a university president. God allowed me to begin fulfilling that dream in 2007 as president of Northwest University in Kirkland, Washington. I have other ambitious dreams I'll be working on for the next twenty-five years as well.

Along with such dreams I set some specific goals. In my early twenties, I set a goal to achieve a doctoral degree from an Ivy League university (doctor of education, Columbia University, 1999). I set a goal to write books. I set a goal to learn to speak Spanish fluently and to be able to read the Greek language of the New Testament. I set a goal to own a home. I set a goal to prosper financially and be able to share with others. I have failed to achieve some of my goals and dreams, and I have not yet fully attempted others. But one thing I have clearly in mind: Achieving my deep dream doesn't depend on reaching every goal I set or every dream I imagine. I can succeed in fulfilling my deep dream even while failing at some of my goals and dreams. Again, *specific goals or dreams are the images that make up our deep dream and suggest its meaning.* They are not the meaning of the dream.

Deep dreams can't be as simple as being a professional athlete or movie star or CEO of a Fortune 500 corporation. They can't be about marrying John or Jane Somebody-in-Particular. They can't be made of dollar amounts or house sizes or the make of a car. All these things are too small to sustain the grandeur of a human dream. Dreams have to be about the kind of person you are going to become and what priorities you are going to pursue in your life. They have to be about something *big*—they have to be a moral vision. Corazon Aquino knew that her dream was about more than just having babies and raising them. She dreamed of truly being a *mother*, fulfilling all the dignity and integrity and strength that define that status. Becoming the mother of her nation was just the consequence of being that person.

My deep dream is not to be a university president. My God-given deep dream is to walk boldly and passionately in obedience to God and to live in such a way that I do not miss out on God's promises to me. When I was nineteen, I promised God I would obey the Holy Spirit's leading in my life, no matter what. I don't always get that right, but I have found the greatest fulfillment in life when I know I am walking in God's will. I pray that no matter what it costs me, I will always try to obey the Lord. That is the only way I will ever know and fulfill my destiny and potential. It is the only way I, a Joseph, can truly prosper and be fulfilled.

Write this down so that you can affirm it: "My dream can never be fulfilled unless it will fulfill me." Go ahead and write it here so you can nail it down a little tighter in your mind.

You will never fulfill your dreams if your dreams don't fulfill you. All an unworthy dream can really be is a gallows for you to hang on. Ugh! Can you see a picture of that? Can you imagine being tortured on the wheel of your own ambitions? That's what will happen if you dream an ignoble dream, one that isn't worthy of you. True humility means knowing who you are and settling for nothing less. It also means setting your sights on things that are appropriate for who you are. Dreams that are *fulfilling* are always dreams that you *can accomplish*.

An amazing truth is implicit in what I just said: If you have set your dream on something you *cannot* accomplish, you have probably set your sights on something that would destroy you if you *did* accomplish it. Humility is the appropriate posture for dreamers. Set your dreams on things you can accomplish, because they truly express your moral and spiritual potential and can thus fill your life with meaning and satisfaction.

GO DEEPER

1. Earlier in this chapter, you read about how I discovered a deep dream based on a sense of who I am. You can do the same. This is no time for false humility, but rather, time for true humility that recognizes who you are. Fill in the blanks in the following statements. In the first blank, you should list something you love. In the second blank, you should write something you plan to do (or already do) to pursue what you love.

- Because I _____,
  I will _____.

- Because I _____,
  I will _____.

- Because I _____,
  I will _____.

- Because I _____,
  I will _____.

- Because I _____,
  I will _____.

You can add more of these kinds of statements in your notebook.

2. Out of the things you are and the things you want to do, you will put together the elements of a deep dream. Take time to imagine yourself doing these things. This may be the first time anyone has given you permission to daydream. Go ahead and spend a few minutes daydreaming about what you want your life to become.

3. What do all the elements of your dream add up to? What is the true essence of your deep dream? What is the one thing you must succeed at to fulfill your God-given destiny? You may not know it yet, but thinking about it will help you define it eventually. Until you do define it, walk out those goals and dreams!

CHAPTER 9

BE TENACIOUS

President Teddy Roosevelt is known as one of the greatest dreamers ever to occupy the White House. Confronting chronic illness as a youth, he dreamed of being a strong and fearless man. At an early age, he determined to build up his body and face down his fears. When he was old enough to leave home, he left his upper-crust New York family and moved out to the wild American West to become a cowboy. Later he would put together a group of like-minded adventurers called the Rough Riders and gain fame and glory as a hero in the Spanish-American War.

When, after the assassination of William McKinley, Roosevelt became the youngest president in American history, he took on the project of building the Panama Canal. The world's richest and most advanced nations had tried and failed to build the canal, but Roosevelt believed in the greatness of America. He took on what seemed like an impossible task. And he built the canal.

In 1948 Leigh Mercer published an ingenious palindrome in tribute to Roosevelt's achievement: "A man, a plan, a canal — Panama."[1] A palindrome is a sentence or phrase that, when read backward, has the same words as when it is read in the usual forward direction. Whether you read the phrase

"A man, a plan, a canal — Panama" from front to back or back to front, it says the same thing. The palindrome seems almost like a mystical sign that Roosevelt was destined to succeed where others had failed.

Many critics thought Roosevelt was crazy, but he pressed on, fearlessly believing it was his destiny to succeed where other leaders had colossally failed. Over twenty-five thousand people died trying to build the canal — some five hundred deaths per mile of construction.[2] Roosevelt's plan for constructing the canal was like the palindrome: It involved starting on both ends and meeting in the middle. Going and coming, front to back and back to front, Roosevelt wholeheartedly committed himself and his nation to building the canal.

He is famous for the following words (please pardon his overuse of the word *man* and read it to include women, too):

> *It is not the critic who counts: not the man who points out how the strong man stumbles or where the doer of deeds could have done better. The credit belongs to the man who is actually in the arena, whose face is marred by dust and sweat and blood, who strives valiantly, who errs and comes up short again and again, because there is no effort without error or shortcoming, but who knows the great enthusiasms, the great devotions, who spends himself for a worthy cause; who, at the best, knows, in the end, the triumph of high achievement, and who, at the worst, if he fails, at least he fails while daring greatly, so that his place shall never be with those cold and timid souls who knew neither victory nor defeat.*[3]

No one who gives something his or her best try is a failure. The real failures are those who fail to try.

Another great example of a dreamer who has never quit is

Philip Anschutz, whose dream included, among other things, serving God through his business career. He is known in the business world today not only as one of the world's richest people, but also as one of the most tenacious. His road to status as a self-made billionaire has been paved with setbacks and dilemmas. From the beginning of his career, he has literally been tried by fire. In 1967, he was working as a wildcatter in Wyoming. After spending everything he had digging speculative oil wells, Anschutz finally struck oil. But right away, the well caught fire and he did not have enough money to put it out. His long-sought, newfound fortune was going up in smoke.

A lot of people would have thrown up their hands and quit at that point. But Anschutz came up with an answer. He had heard that a Hollywood studio was making a movie about Red Adair, the famous oil firefighter. So Anschutz called up the filmmaker and offered to let him film the fire for a fee. Then he used the $100,000 he got from the moviemaker to hire Red Adair to put out the fire.[4] He turned his problem into its own solution.

On the road to becoming a billionaire for the glory of God, Anschutz faced some daunting challenges. He explains his success by saying, "It is only by sticking to an objective through adversity that a goal can ever be realized."[5]

While achieving goals is not the same thing as fulfilling a deep dream, dreams do indeed include the element of accomplishing goals. According to psychologists Abraham Maslow, Erik Erikson, and others, we have to accomplish a few things in order to build the self-esteem we need. Accomplishing goals, especially early in life, is part of what gives us a sense of who we are and what we can indeed do.

Unfortunately, we will fail at a few things. But failing is a huge part of success. Because everyone fails, getting up from failure and continuing on is the very thing that makes success possible. I like what the apostle Paul said in Philippians 3:13-15: "One thing I do: forgetting what lies behind and straining forward to what lies ahead, I press on toward the goal for the prize of the upward call of God in Christ Jesus. Let those of us who are mature think this way." In other words, overcoming the desire to quit after a failure is something we should learn when we are children. Pressing on in spite of failure is a mark of true maturity.

In order to accomplish the goals that undergird your deep dream, you will need some steely minded tenacity. The word *tenacity* comes from a Latin word meaning "to hold on tight." In Spanish, the word *tenaces* means "pliers." Imagine the vice-like grip of a set of forged-steel pliers, holding on tight. Picture a terrier with his teeth sunk into something. Picture a snapping turtle. My very southern daddy told me as a child in Alabama that if a snapping turtle bites you, it won't let go "till it thunders." That snapping turtle mentality is essential for all who would achieve a dream. You've got to grab onto that thing and refuse to let it go.

There is a popular cartoon—photocopied on virtually every copy machine in America—that expresses the concept powerfully. In it, a heron has caught a frog and is trying to swallow him. The frog, on the other hand, has grabbed the heron by the throat and is squeezing so hard the heron can't breathe. The caption says, "Never let go!" That cartoon is a great lesson for dreamers. Many predators will try to swallow you up into their own selfish pursuits. But they can never swallow you up without your permission. If the frog holds on, the heron will conclude there may be another victim that will not be as much trouble to swallow as the frog. Eventually the predator will decide that breathing is a more basic need than eating. (Go ahead and hold your breath. See which comes first, hunger or the desire to breathe!)

The lessons of the cartoon go on and on. There is a great deal of difference between dreamers and predators. Predators are people who are out to use others selfishly to reach their goals. They may indeed reach their goals by that method. But as I've said, they will never be fulfilled human beings. They may turn themselves into horrible monsters that way, but if they prey on others, they will never fulfill their deepest dream. Dreams can only be fulfilled as we include selfless service to others on the way to achieving our dream.

Predators are just bullies. Never let them destroy your dreams. The late country comedian Jerry Clower used to tell the story of a bully who was going around at a party taking down a list of people's names. When asked why he was taking down the names, the bully explained he was making a list of the people he could "whup." One fellow, upon hearing the reason for the list, began to resent the tough guy's attitude. He finally went over to the man and said, "Hey, I'm not so sure you can whup me!" The bully responded by saying, "Well, excuse me, sir. Let me strike your name off my list!"[6]

Most bullies and predators will leave people alone who will stand up to them. While it is important to serve others, it is not good to let yourself become a doormat for people to step all over. That does not contribute to achieving your dream. Such servile sycophancy robs you of your dignity and does not help you gain allies in the fulfillment of your dreams. Predators will not remember the kindnesses of people they consider to be inferior to them. Predatory people are not, however, the only barrier in the way of those trying to fulfill their dreams.

Negative voices can be another big obstacle. Such people can be like the barking dog in the manger — "He won't eat, and he won't let anyone else eat." Naysayers never have a positive word. They say no because they have no faith in you or anyone else. But other negative voices — the voices of truth tellers — say no in order to save you from the disastrous pursuit of an inappropriate dream. While listening to the naysayer can snuff out the light of life, listening to the truth teller can spark the flame of a fire that will be light and warmth to you for years. Listening to the naysayer will drag you down into a pit. Listening to the wise voice of the truth teller will tether you to the ground of reality. It is crucial to know which is which.

So how do you know who is the naysayer and who is the truth teller? The answer is simpler than you may suspect. Naysayers pooh-pooh everyone's dream. They don't believe in anyone. They always say no. They never get excited about anything. They may love you very much. In their peanut-sized imaginations they may think they are protecting your best interests. But they should be the last people to hear about your dreams. You should never listen to them.

The voice of truth, on the other hand, belongs to other dreamers. When other people who have achieved their dreams caution you about the wisdom of an idea, goal, or project you want to pursue, they have earned the right to be heard. While the "no" of the naysayer is poison, the "no" of the truth teller is the nectar of wisdom. Truth tellers recognize unrealistic fantasies because on the way to becoming successful dreamers, they had a few fantasies themselves. When a successful dreamer who loves you tells you your idea will not work, you need to strongly consider taking that advice and moving on to the next idea.

Once you have settled on the deep dream that you know to be the purpose of your life, never, ever, ever consider giving it up. Not until you stand over the cold ashes of your best efforts, having combed through them with your bare hands in search of one more warm spot, one more coal that might be breathed back into an ember with your last hoarse whisper. Only then should you move on, knowing you did your absolute best and walking away with dignity and integrity.

Not only will people and events and circumstances arise over and over to challenge you, *they will even conspire against you*. Remember this: If the fulfillment of dreams were easy, the world would be full of happy, fulfilled people instead of being full of quietly desperate people. Old age would be universally celebrated as the age of honored afterglow instead of being dreaded as an awful dead end. The majority of people will not die happy, and if you are going to avoid being part of that great dark cloud, you had better stay on the sunny side. Never even consider quitting. The only acceptable ending is a dignified retirement after you have either achieved your goals and dreams or failed in a noble, all-out effort that left no excuses.

Words from one of Winston Churchill's most famous speeches must serve as your watchword. During World War II, while England was being mercilessly bombed by the Nazi Luftwaffe, Churchill was scheduled to speak at Harrow School, where he had studied as a boy. Among the words he shared with the students and faculty who gathered were these:

> *Never give in. Never give in. Never, never, never, never — in nothing, great or small, large or petty — never give in, except to convictions of honor and good sense. Never yield to force. Never yield to the apparently overwhelming might of the enemy.*[7]

This spontaneous part of Churchill's speech was inspired by a phrase from a new verse the students had added to one of the old, traditional songs they sang in his honor. The new verse said, in reference to Churchill's leadership, "Not less we praise in darker days." Churchill asked the school's headmaster for permission to change the verse. He said,

> *Do not let us speak of darker days: let us speak rather of sterner days. These are not dark days; these are great days — the greatest days our country has ever lived; and we must all thank God that we have been allowed . . . to play a part in making these days memorable in the history of our race.* [8]

A legend grew up around the speech, which I believed until I took the trouble to look up Churchill's exact words. According to the legend, Churchill stood up and simply said, "Never, never, never give up." The truth is that he said a lot more.

It is good that our culture has preserved the essence of what Churchill said that day so long ago. It would be better still if you would remember some of the rest of what he said. The days that seem the darkest in your life can turn out to be your finest hours. The difference between the hour that defeated you and the hour in which you won the crucial victory of your life will not be determined by something outside of you or beyond your control. Victory and defeat will be determined by the character you take with you into the hardest times, and the tenacity with which you cling to your ideals.

GO DEEPER

1. Make a list of the most important goals you are currently pursuing on your way to fulfilling your deep dream. If you are not currently pursuing any goals, list a few goals you would like to pursue.

a. _____

b. _____

c. _____

d. _____

e. _____

2. Make a list of the predators in your life who would actively try to stop you from achieving these goals. (I hope there are too many blanks here!)

a. _____

b. _____

c. _____

d. _____

e. _____

Is it possible for you to drop any of these people from your life? You should not tolerate the presence of predators in your life if you can possibly get rid of them. It is amazing how many of us tolerate dangerous people in our lives when we do not have to. If there are predators you cannot eliminate from your life, you need to identify them and plan for how you are going to neutralize their harmful effects on you and your plans.

3. Who are the naysayers in your life? (If you write their names down, do it without a label and don't do it here!) Remember, these are negative people who tell you that you cannot do what you desire to do, cannot live a fulfilling life, cannot do anything worthwhile. These are people who must be pushed out of your life or ignored. You cannot allow their opinions to matter to you. Spend as little time with them as you can manage. If this person is your wife or husband or a parent, it may be difficult, but God will help you find a way to be loyal to them without following their bad advice.

4. Who are the truth tellers in your life? These are the people you want to be like. They are successful dreamers, and you want to spend as much time around them as possible. Watch them and learn from them.

a. _____

b. _____

c. _____

d. _____

e. _____

CHAPTER 10

KEEP A FORGIVING SPIRIT

One of the great stories of forgiveness in our time is that of Elisabeth Elliot. Born the daughter of missionaries in Europe, she was raised in a home full of virtue and good character. While in college, she began to realize that God was calling her to become a missionary. She enjoyed studying languages and felt called to be a Bible translator among peoples who had never heard about Christ. Then, in her senior year at Wheaton College, she fell in love with the handsome Jim Elliot, a young man who was unusually dedicated to God and was also called to missionary work.

For Jim and Elisabeth, it was not enough just to fall in love. They wisely understood that "falling in love" is not a good enough reason to get married.[1] They felt they must follow God's leading instead. So each followed God for the next five years and wound up serving in Ecuador among two different indigenous people groups. As their ministries diverged and coincided, a time came when they were living across the street from each other in Quito. Jim commented at the time, "Dreams are tawdry when compared with the leading of God, and not worthy of the aura of wonder we usually surround them with.

God only doeth wonders. He does nothing else."[2]

Finally convinced that God was leading the two of them to wed, they were married in 1953.[3] Two years later, the couple had a baby daughter, and it seemed that Elisabeth's dreams of being a missionary linguist, marrying Jim, and having a family were coming true. Though she had always been willing to sacrifice her dreams to the will of God, she finally had things she had dreamed of for years.[4]

Just ten months later, Jim and four other missionaries decided to reach out to the Huaorani, a remote and primitive jungle tribe formerly called Aucas.[5] The Huaorani were famous for being hostile to outsiders. In all fairness, they had plenty of reason to be concerned about the intentions of outsiders. Despite the danger, Jim and his friends flew a small plane into the jungle and landed along a riverbank, determined to meet the Huaorani in their own territory. Six days later, the men were found dead, speared to death.

Often a missionary returns home when a spouse has died. Everyone understands the need to return to the security and support of family. But Elisabeth's dream of serving Christ as a missionary was not dependent on her marriage to Jim, and keeping her dream alive forced her to truly heroic depths. Just as Hebrews 2:10 says that Jesus Christ, "the founder of [our] salvation," was made "perfect through suffering," Elisabeth found that following Christ would imply deep suffering in her own life, and the death of her husband would not kill her dream.

Shortly after Jim's death, Elisabeth met two Huaorani women who had left their homes in the jungle. Seeing their need, she took them into her house and befriended them. Befriending any Huaorani person was a clear act of forgiveness, but Elisabeth understood it was only a beginning. In order to honor her husband's sacrifice, she would have to do much more. She and her daughter, along with Rachel Saint, whose brother had been killed alongside Jim, learned the language of the Huaorani from the two houseguests. Just a short time after Jim's death, the three missionaries were able to go peacefully into a Huaorani village and tell the people about their faith in Jesus Christ.[6]

As Elisabeth met the six men who had killed her husband and his friends, she was forced to recognize their humanity. It is easy to dehumanize people who have hurt us and turn them into monsters in our minds. But instead of doing the easy thing, Elisabeth offered her friendship to the men. One of them explained to her that he had thought outsiders would kill and eat the Huaorani. Given the history of European encroachments on indigenous people in the Americas, it was not a ridiculous fear. Another man told her he had cried after the killings.

Because of Elisabeth's forgiveness, all six of the killers became Christians, and one of them, a man named Kimo, became the pastor of the village church that Elisabeth and Rachel founded. All the men became close friends to Elisabeth and her daughter. Though Elisabeth returned to the United States after two years, Rachel stayed behind to translate the New Testament into the Huaorani language. Today, many of the Huaorani people are Christians.[7]

If Elisabeth had refused to forgive the Huaorani, her husband's death would have been in vain. She would probably have lived the rest of her life in an endless nightmare of bitterness. But her forgiveness of her husband's murderers, followed by love and friendship for them, confirmed the truth of her message that God offers forgiveness to sinful and broken humanity, not in spite of the murder of Jesus Christ but *through*

it. Elisabeth's life of forgiveness not only resulted in reconciliation but also established her as a virtuous role model for
generations of men and women who have read her books and
listened to her teaching.

Elisabeth Elliot has fulfilled many goals and dreams over
her long life — graduating from Wheaton, becoming a missionary linguist, marrying Jim Elliot, becoming a mother,
blessing the world through her books — but none of these
things was her deep dream. From the outside looking in, I think
Elisabeth's deep dream was what Thomas à Kempis called "the
imitation of Christ." If she had fulfilled all of her goals but had
not forgiven those who had hurt her so deeply and taken away
the life she had dreamed of, she would have failed to be like
Jesus. The fulfillment of her desire to follow him with her whole
heart and life has led many people to see her as one of the most
Christlike figures of our time.

Would you have been able to forgive the Huaorani men? It
is likely that someone has hurt or wronged you, and it is hard to
forgive people, especially those who have neither confessed nor
repented of their offenses against you. Such people do not
deserve forgiveness. In fact, they deserve to have bitter revenge
visited upon them. In a sense, it may seem like injustice to
forgive people who do not deserve forgiveness. But the problem
is that all of us want to be forgiven when we hurt others, whether
we deserve it or not.

In the end, we should realize that forgiveness has little to do
with the people who have hurt us and everything to do with
healing the wounds they have inflicted on our lives so that they
cannot continue to hurt us. As long as we hate people, as long
as we continue to nurse grudges against them, their offenses
against us remain a hurtful part of our lives and continue to

plague us. But as soon as we manage to forgive them, we free ourselves from their hold on us.

In most cases, our refusal to forgive others has little effect on them and a crippling effect on us. So why do we want to hang onto feelings of unforgiveness? As a pastor, I have seen people stubbornly refuse to forgive someone, even though the memory of what that person did was still destroying their lives many years after the offense. It is a terrible thing to witness.

I think people do not want to forgive others because they mistakenly believe one of the following lies:

- *By withholding forgiveness, I can make the person who wronged me suffer.* The truth is that offenders often could not care less whether or not we forgive them. Some people get perverse pleasure from hurting others. Universally, the person who is most hurt by unforgiveness is the person who harbors it.
- *If I forgive someone, God won't punish him or her.* The truth is that you can be sure each person will pay for his or her sins—and that includes you. We all reap what we sow, and it is best to keep that in mind when choosing whether to sow forgiveness.[8] All of us really need the grace of God, which is indeed our only hope of escaping the full penalty of our sins.
- *If I forgive people, I have to go back to liking, trusting, or spending time with them.* The truth is that forgiving people does not imply liking, trusting, or returning to close relationship with them. In most cases, the relationship with a person who has deeply wounded you will be permanently damaged, and you will move on to other relationships. There are, however, cases where

forgiveness leads to full reconciliation. When that happens, it is a beautiful thing, not something to dread. Often, such reconciliations are crucial to the fulfillment of your deep dream. One factor to consider in deciding whether to return gradually to a closer relationship with such a person is the overall importance of that person in your deep dream. A spouse is worthy of much deeper consideration than an acquaintance, coworker, or friend.

- *If I forgive people, it will be more likely that they will hurt me again.* In many cases, we will not easily give people a chance to hurt us again because, even if we have forgiven them, they must regain our trust through right behavior. The fact that you have forgiven someone does not mean you have to become gullible or foolish toward that person. The key to full reconciliation is the offending person's full *repentance*. If the one who has hurt you is not truly sorry and does not try to make amends, it is likely that person will continue hurting you. If people continue acting against you, you can and should put distance between yourself and them. You are not required to let them hurt you. You are only required to release your hatred and any desire for revenge, remaining open to reconciliation if the offenders should come to their senses and abandon their hurtful behavior.

The main point I want to make is that forgiveness lightens the load we carry through life. High achievers do not climb to the pinnacle of success while carrying a heavy pack of offenses. They learn to travel light and move on to the next thing. If they remember past offenses, they do so in terms of how those offenses may be useful to them in climbing higher.

Imagine a mountain climber who is finally scaling a peak after an arduous ascent. Imagine that she has done the whole thing with a huge, heavy pack on her back. Now imagine that just as she is making that last difficult reach to get over a final cliff that keeps her from the top, her heavy pack upsets her balance and she tumbles backward, falling off the cliff to her ruin. It is an apt picture of the destructive power of vengeance, but it would be a rare one. Most people carrying that pack will never come anywhere close to the top.

To overcome your enemies, keep a clear heart and a forgiving spirit. At the crowning moment of success in achieving your dream, when you are celebrating all of God's blessings on your life, you do not want the demons of unforgiveness on your guest list. They will keep that party from ever happening.

I believe you will never be able to develop the habit of forgiving other people until you have first experienced forgiveness. Only people who know they have been forgiven by others will find the strength to make a habit of forgiving. Here are three things you can do to become a forgiving person:

1. Recognize any way you have failed God, and ask God to forgive you. This failure may be something as simple as not accepting yourself for who you are. It may involve the cowardice of shrinking back from doing the things you believe you were born to do. It is likely that you have not thought about it this way, but it is a sin against God and yourself if you fail to pursue your deep dream.

It is often said that one of the original meanings of the word *sin* has to do with "missing the mark." At its heart, sin means falling short of God's ideal — like an arrow that falls short of its target. If God created you, you have to know yourself and love yourself. If God has a plan for your life, you have to devote yourself to realizing that plan. If God has given you a dream to fulfill, then it is an act of ingratitude not to pursue it. The ultimate sin is to fall short of the target God has designed you to achieve.

Romans 3:23 says that "all have sinned and fall short of the glory of God." What does it mean to fall short of God's glory? I do not think that phrase means we have failed to be as glorious as God is. Obviously, no created thing can be as great as the one who created it. If that were the meaning of "falling short of God's glory," we would be sinful for the very fact of existing. That simply cannot be the case, because if it were, we would be beyond all redemption and God would be a monster for having created us at all.

I think the phrase refers to our failure to achieve the glory God has planned for us. Falling short of our potential is a serious failure. The fact that we all fall short of our glorious potential means that we need God's forgiveness to reach the ultimate human potential—attaining eternal life in heaven. Even if we ultimately fail to achieve the earthly life God designed us for, it is never too late in this life to gain a place in heaven. Still, falling short of our God-given destiny in this life is too costly in the here and now for us to abandon it. If you know you have fallen short of God's glorious ideal for your life, ask God to forgive you for everything you have done wrong. Doing so will result in a great sense of relief in your life, and will also prepare you for step two in becoming a forgiving person.

2. Forgive yourself. If you know God has forgiven you for every wrong that you have done, then you have no reason not to forgive yourself. One of the saddest things you ever hear is when a person says, "I can never forgive myself for X." Whenever I hear people say that, I know that they—and everyone around them—are in for a difficult future. Have you ever met people who were hard on themselves but gracious toward others? I have not. I don't want certain people to love me as they love themselves. Believe me, if people around you are hoping you won't love them as you love yourself, you need to change! You need to forgive yourself and find the power to love yourself. If you do that, you will find the power to love other people and forgive them.

3. Ask for forgiveness from people you have wronged. Receiving forgiveness from these people will remove any excuse you may be using to justify your unforgiveness of others. It may be that other people will not want to forgive you, but the fact that you have apologized and asked for their forgiveness sets you free from the reality of guilt. Obviously, this is only true if you have stopped doing whatever you are apologizing for.

It may take time for people to see your sincerity and choose to forgive you. But there is great dignity for you in asking others to forgive you. You are asking them to do something that will bring enormous relief and help into their lives. If they choose not to do so, it will not be your fault. Give them time and space, and do everything you can to make up for what you did wrong. If you do this, you will find that you are free from guilt.

Taking these three steps of forgiveness will remove enormous obstacles from your life that could keep you from fulfilling your dreams. But there may be one other kind of forgiveness you have to take care of before you can even begin the other three steps. It may be that you need to forgive God.

Many people blame God for bad things that have happened to them. Their response to tragedy or setbacks has been to refuse to believe in God anymore. In some ways this is a good thing. They need to reject the god they believed in before tragedy struck, because they were believing in a false god.

Many people—even Christians—have a twisted picture of who God is. They think God's job is to protect them and keep anything bad from happening to them. Their prayers are a list of petitions they want God to grant them. They behave as if the only thing that separates God from Santa Claus is that Santa only has to perform once a year. These people want God to shower gifts on them every day. It never occurs to them to ask what they ought to give God. Their picture of deity is that God is their great cosmic servant, like Aladdin's genie.

God has never offered to be our cosmic servant. In fact, God demands the exact opposite—to be our cosmic Lord.[9] We are built to serve God, not the other way around. Our question should not be how God can serve us, but rather, how we can serve God. When we have an adequate picture of God and realize we are here to do God's work, our lives take on a whole new meaning.

Some people are deeply disappointed in God for not being their cosmic servant and caretaker. They need to forgive God, not for God's benefit but for their own good. They need to pour out the emotions of bitterness that have built up over their disappointment with God. When they do forgive God and invite him into their lives as Lord instead of servant, God can become real to them. They can know God and be transformed by that knowledge—as we saw in chapter 3. When that happens, they will immediately perceive the greatness of God and realize how foolish they were to expect God to be their genie. Out of that perception of God's greatness comes worship and praise of God and a willingness to do anything, endure anything, suffer anything, in order to be with God now and forever.

To be with God is really the truest dream of every human

being. It is the greatest purpose for which we were made. Every worthy dream on earth is just a seed of that ultimate destiny. Even unworthy dreams are twisted versions of our truest dream. We can achieve it through God's forgiveness — in our lives and, through us, in the people who have wronged us.

GO DEEPER

1. Is there anything in your life that makes you angry or bitter at God? Is there something you need to forgive God for? If so, confess that thing now and forgive God for it. In your own words, recognize before God that you have had bitter feelings, and ask God to be present in your life. Remember that Jesus not only bore your sins on the cross, but your sorrows as well.[10] He understands our suffering because he shared in it.

2. Confess to God that you have sinned and fallen short of your own goals. Tell God that you have not become the kind of person you want to be. Confess that you have not achieved the goals you have set for yourself. Ask God to change you and give you power to achieve his plan for your life.

3. Forgive yourself for falling short of your moral goals, your worldly dreams, and your spiritual destiny. Recognize that it was unrealistic for you to achieve these things without God's help. Make a pledge that you will love yourself so you can love God and others the way they deserve to be loved. Write down your own emancipation proclamation, setting yourself free.

4. In your notebook, make a list of people you need to forgive. No matter what they may have done to you, confess out loud that you forgive them. Even if you do not feel like you have forgiven them, go ahead and say it. Feelings will come with time. Go ahead and forgive them, for your own good. Get the

wounds they have caused you out of your life. If you have to do this every day for a while, go ahead and do it until you feel free from the injury they have done to you. If you truly think they will benefit from knowing that you have forgiven them, you may want to call or meet with them to effect reconciliation.

CHAPTER 11

KEEP A POSITIVE OUTLOOK

I n September 2002, the world lost one of its all-time great positive thinkers with the death—at age one hundred—of W. Clement Stone. To say that Stone was a self-made man is to insult him with faint praise. He was a self-made child! When he was only three years old, his father died, leaving the family nothing but debts. By the age of six, little Clement was already at work, selling newspapers on the street corners of Chicago.[1] Child labor laws and today's American culture would suggest that poor little Clement was being exploited, but he did not see it that way. He saw himself as a serious businessman, and by the age of thirteen he owned his own newsstand on the South Side of Chicago.

Though his father was a gambler and a loser, his mother became a disciplined businesswoman after being left alone. With Clement succeeding in Chicago, she moved to Detroit to start an insurance agency. At sixteen, Clement followed her there and began to sell insurance. He approached sales with a positive outlook. What others called "cold calls" he called "gold calls."[2] Four years later, as a high school dropout with a total savings of $100, he opened his own insurance agency, and within eight years he had a thousand agents working for him. Before long, he became a multimillionaire. Over the course of his lifetime, he gave over $275 million to charity, making him one of the most generous philanthropists in history. The secret to W. Clement Stone's success was something he called "positive mental attitude." In his final interview with the press, Stone attributed his philosophy to the fact that as a twelve-year-old, he read over fifty Horatio Alger novels in a single summer.[3] Horatio Alger was the author of about 135 "dime novels," popular at the turn of the twentieth century, which always featured poor boys who became successful by cultivating good character, working hard, obeying the Golden Rule, and always doing the right thing. Stone put those principles to work in his own life, and he became a great success.

Another important influence on Stone was Napoleon Hill. In 1908 the great businessman and philanthropist Andrew Carnegie commissioned Hill to discover and communicate the principles of success. Hill's books helped Stone discover the principles of positive mental attitude that eventually turned his $100 savings into an insurance empire worth over $2 billion.

W. Clement Stone made it his life's work to help other people succeed. In his early years in the insurance business, he specialized in taking in poor and uneducated people, teaching them a simple and positive sales philosophy, and helping them become successful insurance agents. The first time I ever heard of Clement Stone was when I read David Wilkerson's book *The Cross and the Switchblade*. Wilkerson's book tells the story of Teen Challenge, one of the world's most successful rehabilitation programs for drug addicts.[4] Stone was one of the first major donors and board members of Teen Challenge, contributing heavily to helping many hopeless drug addicts find their way out of addiction and into productive lives full of faith in God.

A few quotations from W. Clement Stone neatly illustrate his philosophy of positive mental attitude:

Aim for the moon. If you miss, you may hit a star.

All personal achievement starts in the mind of the individual. Your personal achievement starts in your mind. The first step is to know exactly what your problem, goal or desire is.

Bondage is subjection to external influences and internal negative thoughts and attitudes.

Have the courage to say no. Have the courage to face the truth. Do the right thing because it is right. These are the magic keys to living your life with integrity.

Like success, failure is many things to many people. With Positive Mental Attitude, failure is a learning experience, a rung on the ladder, a plateau at which to get your thoughts in order and prepare to try again.

Prayer is man's greatest power!

Regardless of who you are or what you have been, you can be what you want to be.

Whatever the mind of man can conceive and believe, it can achieve.[5]

During the prosperous 1950s and 1960s, a huge "positive-thinking movement" grew up in America around writers like Stone and Hill. Mainline Protestant ministers such as Norman Vincent Peale and, later, Robert Schuller were also preaching the virtues of positive thinking. In other Christian circles, a similar philosophy arose, called by its critics the "Positive Confession Movement." Sometimes Christian positive thinkers seemed to be preaching faith in faith more than faith in God. The more extreme proponents of the positive-thinking movement sometimes left God out completely. Faith in faith can take you a long way, but it is a poor substitute for faith in God. Such thinking certainly went in a different direction from Clement Stone.

Positive thinking is indeed powerful, but there is a limit to being positive. That limit was brilliantly revealed by one of America's most unusual thinkers, the late Moe Howard. In one of his popular Three Stooges comedies, Moe says, "Only fools are positive." His friend Larry Fine asks, "Are you sure?" and Moe responds, "I'm positive."[6] Being positive about the wrong thing can make a fool out of you.

While thinking positively can contribute enormously to success, it is not enough to guarantee success. I have met many people who believed in positive confession in such a way that caused them not to face facts. Lying to ourselves—no matter how positive the lie—is not wise. It is essential to think positively about the right things, otherwise we may accomplish the wrong things.

In the previous chapter, I said that a lot of people harbor bitter feelings toward God and need to forgive God for not living up to their expectations. The reason they are in this position is simple: They have misunderstood how God works in the midst of evil. Such misunderstandings are easy to comprehend. Theologians and philosophers have been trying to grasp God's relationship to evil since human beings first came to a knowledge of what evil is. I certainly do not pretend to understand that mystery fully. But I stand on what Joseph of Egypt pointed out to his brothers about God and evil after their father's death: "Don't be afraid. Am I in the place of God? You intended to harm me, but God intended it for good to accomplish what is now being done, the saving of many lives."[7] Joseph understood the unspeakable evil human beings are capable of planning and carrying out. But he also understood that they do not have the final word.

God has given humanity the greatest force for either good or ill that exists—a free will. God knew such a gift had the potential for great harm, but with sovereignty and foresight, he always plans a way to weave even the most evil human acts back into the divine plan and to transform those evil acts for our good. Joseph knew that no matter what evil men or women might plan against him, God would turn it back to achieve God's own purposes.

Sometimes it seems that nature itself, including fundamental things like time and space, conspires against us. To explain why would take us further into complex theology than this book is designed to go. Even if we were to explore that answer in detail, I can tell you it would not bring a lot of comfort to people who are grieving. Our problem is not that we do not understand why tragedies occur. The issue is not philosophical. The issue is the personal loss we have suffered. No mere "reason" can make us whole while we are in the grip of grief.

Whatever the ultimate cosmic reasons for human suffering may be, the bottom line is that those who love God are not alone in the midst of it. God is there for us, and he is not idle. No matter what evil thing may happen to us, God is creating a path that will bring us back to our divine destiny. Not only will he make a way for us to arrive at our destination, he promises to make us better for having to get there by a hard road.

The apostle Paul knew God works that way: "And we know

that in all things God works for the good of those who love him, who have been called according to his purpose."[8] People who love God should also know that he will always be at work to resolve their problems. Even when the worst attacks, the vilest betrayals, and the gravest offenses threaten our dreams and even our lives, God is at work *in defense of those who love him.* The greatest defense against evil is for us to love God. Remember this: The greatest commandment in the Bible is the command to love God with all of our heart, soul, mind, and strength.[9] Obeying that command means never being defenseless in the face of our problems.

Have you ever asked why God commands us to love him? For that matter, one might ask why God would command us to do anything. God is infinitely greater than we are, and we are — at least in terms of size — like mere quarks in a universe that is immense beyond our imagination. Why does God care whether we love him or whether we do the things he likes? How does it help God at all if we love or obey him?

The answer is that God does not need our love or obedience. We need to love and obey God. God has given us precious commandments for *our* good. Note the term *precious* here. All of God's commandments—love the Lord your God, honor your father and mother, do not kill, steal, commit adultery, or covet, make no idols, and all the other commandments—are precious.[10] So many people act as though God is a cosmic kill-joy who is trying to take all the fun out of life. Nothing could be farther from the truth. There is nothing fun or funny about dishonoring our parents, stealing, or committing adultery. Some of these activities may start with a thrill of emotion, but they always end in heartache. As the old saying goes, "Trouble always starts as fun."

We are commanded to love God because he knows that if

we do, we will avoid much trouble and live happier, more fulfilled lives. Unless we love God, there is no way we can be free to fulfill our purpose totally in the world, because the purpose of humanity is to know and love God. Ironically, obedience to God's commands truly makes us free as human beings. As Saint Augustine summarized the matter, "Love God and do as you please." Loving God sanctifies or makes holy all of our other loves. The love of God legitimizes all of our other pursuits. No dream will bring ultimate fulfillment unless it includes the love of God.

When we base our lives on the love of God, his promise that all things work together for good can be fulfilled in our lives. When we know this truth, we can look disaster in the face with confidence and peace. In pain or pleasure, failure or success, poverty or prosperity, in the ugly and the beautiful, God is with us, working out everything for our eternal good.

When we learn to love God as we love ourselves, we can know that he is always working to help us achieve his plan for our lives. Once we know God is with us, we realize we can do anything. The apostle Paul said in Philippians 4:13, "I can do all things through [Christ] who strengthens me." Positive thinking about what we can do is only half the battle. The other half is thinking about the help God will give us. With that help, we can lead a fulfilling life of dreams.

GO DEEPER

1. In your notebook, write out your God-given dream for the life ahead of you. Do not forget to include the moral dimensions of the person you want to become. Don't be afraid to be specific about goals you want to reach. Be sure to take your

personal strengths, talents, pleasures, and interests into account. Include the ways you plan to serve others. Be sure to consult your answers from the previous exercises in writing out your dream.

2. Are you determined to achieve this dream? If so, sign the following confession with a big, bold signature:

I believe God has created me as a special person with a special mission in life. Because of this, I am worthy to achieve the dream God has given me. The dream I have written is a faithful representation of who I am, and with God's help I can achieve it. I am determined to pursue it.

_____

Signature   Date

CHAPTER 12

USING WHAT YOU HAVE TO GET WHAT YOU WANT

I want to leave you with a story that explains one more characteristic dreamers need to develop: *shrewdness*. A lot of people think negatively of shrewdness, interpreting it as a quality that enables a person to cheat others. While some people undoubtedly use craftiness to take advantage of others, that is not the essence of shrewdness. Shrewdness is the maximization of available skills and resources for the optimal achievement of desired results. It is simply the art of using what you have to get what you want.

The success stories of all the world's great dreamers have been characterized by wise and strategic use of resources. I could spend many pages telling you about the shrewd leaders and achievers of history, but I am afraid that by doing so, I might make it sound as if you have to be famous in order to achieve your deep dream. So let me just tell you a story about an ordinary person who was a successful dreamer.

Nancy Carroll was poor, uneducated, skinny, and plain. She didn't want a lot, just a Little. Specifically, she wanted

Enoch Little, a young man from her community. The story of how she first got Enoch has been lost to history and tradition, but the story of how she got him back will probably live on as long as she has descendants. The bare facts of the story are documented in the Alabama State Archives and in the book *Castleberry and Allied Families,* volume 1.[1]

Nancy married Enoch in 1860 and bore him a baby daughter just a year later. They were dirt-poor southerners trying to scrape out an existence on poor dirt—a hilly plot of east Alabama land unsuited for just about everything except growing soft pine trees and hardy people. They had little practical interest in questions like the liberation or retention of slaves or the right to import goods from Europe instead of the northern states. For her part, Nancy dreamed about being a self-reliant, God-fearing wife and mother with a happy home in the same rural community where she was born. She wanted to be surrounded by her kith and kin, taking care of her husband and her children, with enough prosperity to meet the needs of the people she loved. But that dream was threatened when Enoch "went for a soldier" in 1862.

By late 1864 the South had for all intents and purposes already lost the Civil War. The Southern supply lines had been cut, so things like boots were in short supply. Enoch was like many other soldiers who, in the absence of boots, had wrapped their feet up in cloths to try to give them some protection. One day while charging the enemy in battle, he stepped on a "hack hawthorn" (whatever that was), which slowed him down enough for the Yankees to capture him as a prisoner of war.

Enoch was just a humble private, and when he told his captors he knew nothing, it was likely the gospel truth. Still, his tormentors subjected him to a number of tortures, including tying him over a barrel, face up—with his hands and feet secured to heavy rocks—in order to drip water slowly into his nose. They left him out in the rain, tied up and naked. They drove pins under his toenails to get information out of him. The records of his testimony are still in the Alabama State Archives to document it.

But as we southerners say, "You can't get blood out of a turnip." Enoch had no information to share with the Yankees, and eventually they gave up and left him alone. The wound in his foot, however, got infected, and he became very sick. In early 1865, he was traded back to the South in exchange for some Yankee POWs who had probably suffered the same way he had. As he was extremely ill, he was placed in a hospital in Richmond, Virginia.

Word got back home to Nancy that Enoch was dying in a hospital in Virginia. If she wanted to see him again, she would have to go to him quickly. Both of Enoch's older brothers had already been killed in the war, and Nancy was determined that her man would not join them.

According to legend, she hitched up her wagon and drove it until she could board a flat railway car. She traveled, exposed to the winter weather, for two more days to Richmond. On the third day, she finally saw her dying husband. Nancy's dream was dying too. But she had not come to Virginia to say good-bye to her husband and her dream. She had come to save them. She went to the hospital clerk, a teenage boy with the start of a good education and some talent, and begged him to discharge her husband so she could take him home and nurse him herself.

But there was a problem. As the Southern war effort was hopeless, many soldiers were beginning to desert. To stop these desertions, a rule had been put in place that limited leaves to nine days. The hospital clerk explained to her that because Enoch was a soldier, he could have only nine days of leave.

Nancy protested that it would take her three days to get him home and another three to return. What good would three days at home do her husband? He would probably die on the way and never even get home. The clerk, powerless to help, referred her to the commanding officer of the military hospital.

Nancy boldly presented herself to the commanding officer, who was outdoors walking around instead of working in his office. She explained her situation, but the commander would not give her husband more than nine days of leave. In desperation, she accepted what she could get. The commander wrote a note on brown paper, authorizing the clerk to prepare papers giving Enoch Little nine days of leave.

When the commander finished writing the note and handed it to Nancy, he threw down the stubby pencil he had used and walked away. Nancy, seeing that his back was turned, looked down at the pencil. She looked at her note, and then again at the pencil. Her husband's life and her dream were at stake. Quickly, she grabbed up that pencil and went away to hide for a moment.

Nancy did not have any education, but she did know that a 0 added to a 9 makes 90. I've been told she wasn't sure which side of the 9 to put the 0 on. But she was a woman of faith, and she prayed that God would help her. She quickly wrote a 0 on the right side of the 9 and went back to the teenage hospital clerk.

"Ma'am, I don't know how you got this permission, but that is the commander's signature," said the clerk.

He filled out leave papers for ninety days and Nancy took her husband home. Away from the infection and hopelessness of the hospital, she used a medicine unavailable to the military doctors—the love of a wife. This therapy was just what Enoch needed, and he recovered remarkably.

The war ended before the end of the ninety-day period, and Enoch never had to return to the army. He lived on into the 1890s, never leaving Nancy and his home again.

After the turn of the century, the United States Congress approved a pension for widows of Civil War veterans. As a poor widow, Nancy needed that pension and in 1914 went down to the county courthouse to apply for her benefits. She was shocked to find out she was ineligible due to her husband having been listed as AWOL at the end of the war. Nancy knew that Enoch had indeed been given official leave. She had made out the papers herself! But she had no evidence to prove it. The papers had been destroyed in a house fire in 1876.

As you may expect, Nancy had shown those papers to a lot of people. She went around and collected affidavits from all the old soldiers she knew who had seen the papers (there was an "old-folks home" exclusively for Confederate veterans not far from her home). When she felt she had enough papers to make her case, she went to the county courthouse to file her appeal. When the old county clerk in Rockford, Alabama, looked at the papers, he said, "I remember you. You're the lady who got the miraculous ninety-day leave." About fifty years earlier, he had been a teenage clerk at a Confederate hospital in Virginia. Nancy drew her pension until she died in 1933.

Nancy Little was my great-great-grandmother. Her daughter Rebecca—conceived shortly after Enoch came home from the war—married Joseph Wiley Castleberry, a singing-school teacher who specialized in shaped-note Sacred Harp singing. Had my great-great-grandmother not achieved her goal of saving

Private Enoch, I would never have been born to dream my own dreams. Because she achieved her dream, she made it possible for her children and others associated with her to achieve their own dreams.

She lived out the dream she took responsibility for leading. Though she experienced the heartache, common in her time, of seeing one of her children die young, and even though Enoch died before reaching a ripe old age, she herself lived long and saw several of her grandchildren become respected adults, some of them becoming ministers. Nancy's faith had an impact on her children and their children for generations.

Nancy Little was a shrewd person, and because of it, she achieved her dream. She knew how to use what little she had to achieve her hopes and dreams. All she had was a scrap of paper and a used-up, stubby pencil, but apparently dreams can be saved with such things. She also had the scrappy courage and stubby determination to write a new ending to a life script that didn't match her dreams. Most important, she had faith that God would be with her and give her success in her efforts.

Your dreams and their fulfillment will require no less of you. A few years ago, I saw something that helped me understand godly shrewdness. On a particular night, I was attending the biennial meeting of the Association of Theological Schools. Believe me, it was a dream come true for me to attend that conference as academic dean of a seminary. But as I got out of my hotel to explore the area around it, I saw something that challenged me to keep diving longer, deeper, and clearer into my dreams.

Just a few blocks from my hotel, I explored the grounds of a large and famous church. In the garden I found a statue called *The Smiling Jesus: The Miracle of the Loaves and Fishes*. A happy

Jesus is receiving the five loaves and two fishes from a young boy. The boy did not have much, but he gave Jesus what he had, and Jesus took this small lunch and used it to miraculously feed five thousand people.[2]

The sculptor of *The Smiling Jesus*, John Soderberg, inscribed a message for those who view the art: "Offer your dreams to Christ. Let him take your humble resources and multiply them to enrich the lives of yourself and others. Enter this place of worship and your soul will be fed with Christ's Spirit."

As I stood there, I did just that. I took hold of my dreams and offered them up to Christ. I saw them reflected in the loaves and fishes of the little boy. I saw the smile of Jesus as he rejoiced that I would trust him enough to surrender my dreams to him and let him do with them as he would. I saw my face on the delighted little boy. I entered into a place of worship and into God's presence, and I knew that God would be with me as I live out my dreams and submit my humble resources to him.

If you are shrewd enough to do that too, this book is about you. Not only will you fulfill your deep dream, but you will share it with others and become an ideal guide to them in fulfilling their dream. Your family, your friends, your coworkers—even your competitors and enemies—will one day rise up and call you blessed. Go on! Dive deeper for your dream.

ACKNOWLEDGMENTS

Without my dear friend and *pater libri*, Ted Terry of Collins-Terry Associates, this book would still be nothing more than 0's and 1's in my computer. He never stopped believing in me and then never gave up on the book. I deeply appreciate Don Simpson and all the people at NavPress who adopted this project with refreshing flexibility and vision. Liz Heaney taught me the deep truth of what I had told students for years but now actually understand: "There are no great writers, only great editors." Among them, surely she is the greatest; I pray she will keep working with me as I try to write other books. Tia Stauffer was a patient project manager.

Jim Edwards, my writing professor at Evangel University some thirty years ago, continues to speak to me across the miles and years through critiques of my papers that he has long forgotten but I will remember forever. The faculty of the Assemblies of God Theological Seminary deserves recognition for inspiring me to write while I served as their dean, and they have encouraged me all along the way.

Finally and most important, my wife, Kathleen, and my daughters—Jessica, Jodie, and Sophie—continue to be my greatest support in living the dream from which this book emerged. Let's do it again!

NOTES

Chapter 1: Deep Dreams

1. Mike Tidwell, *Amazon Stranger: A Rainforest Chief Battles Big Oil* (New York: Lyons Press, 1996), 26. A great place to start reading about Randy Borman is the website www.cofan.org. Tidwell's book is a beautifully written, full-length treatment of Borman's early career among the Cofan.
2. Peter K. Austin, ed., *One Thousand Languages: Living, Endangered, and Lost* (Berkeley: University of California Press, 2008).
3. "Gringo Chief Rules Swath of Ecuadorian Jungle," *All Things Considered*, National Public Radio, July 5, 2010.
4. Tidwell, 201.
5. Henry David Thoreau, *Walden* (Boston: Beacon Press, 1854, 2004), 6.
6. E. E. Cummings, *Complete Poems*, vol. 2 (London: MacGibbon & Kee, 1968), 732.

Chapter 2: Know Yourself

1. Viktor Frankl, *Man's Search for Meaning* (New York: Washington Square Press, 1963), 109.
2. Richard Foster, *Celebration of Discipline: The Path to Spiritual Growth* (San Francisco: HarperCollins, 1978), 172.

Chapter 3: Know God

1. Henry George Liddell and Robert Scott, *Greek-English Lexicon, Abridged* (Oxford: Clarendon Press, 1991), 661.
2. Luke 19:8, NIV.
3. *Rudy*, directed by David Anspaugh (TriStar Pictures, 1993).

140   YOUR DEEPEST DREAM

4. Genesis 1:27.
5. Acts 10:38.
6. Matthew 9:35.
7. John 8:3-4,10-11.
8. John 17:8.
9. Hebrews 4:15.
10. John 17:4-5.
11. Matthew 26:57-66; 27:24-26.
12. Isaiah 53:6.
13. 2 Corinthians 5:21.
14. Isaiah 53:4.

Chapter 4: Embrace Your Destiny
1. Edá Kriseová, *Václav Havel: The Authorized Biography*, trans. Caleb Crain (New York: St. Martin's Press, 1993), 13.
2. In addition to Kriseová's authorized biography, information from Havel himself can be found in the fascinating personal interviews in *Disturbing the Peace: A Conversation with Karel Hvížd'ala* (New York: Knopf, 1990).
3. "Václav Havel: Quotes," Goodreads, http://www.goodreads.com/author/quotes/71441.
4. Stephen Hawking, *Black Holes and Baby Universes and Other Essays* (New York: Bantam, 1994), 127–140.
5. "Westminster Shorter Catechism," Center for Reformed Theology and Apologetics, http://www.reformed.org/documents/WSC.html.
6. Ioan James, "Singular Scientists," *Journal of the Royal Society of Medicine* 96, no. 1 (January 2003): 36.

Chapter 5: Be Willing to Be a Leader
1. Stewart Burns, *To the Mountaintop: Martin Luther King Jr.'s Sacred Mission to Save America 1955–1968* (New York: HarperSanFrancisco, 2005), 51.
2. Burns, 56.
3. Deuteronomy 6:5.
4. Mark 12:31.
5. James MacGregor Burns, *Leadership* (New York: Harper & Row, 1978), 33–34.
6. Mark 8:36.

Chapter 6: Be Willing to Serve Others
1. "Father of the River Walk," The Historical Marker Database, http://www.hmdb.org/marker.asp?MarkerID=30606&Print=1.
2. Mark 12:31.

Chapter 7: Live a Life of Integrity
1. Rosa Parks, *Quiet Strength* (Grand Rapids, MI: Zondervan, 1994), 22.
2. Erik Erikson, *Childhood and Society* (New York: Norton, 1950).

Chapter 8: Be Humble
1. Luke 14:11.
2. Philippians 2:9-11.
3. Mel White, *Aquino* (Dallas: Word, 1989), 33–34.
4. Seth Mydans, "Family Vaults Women to Leadership in Asia," *New York Times*, February 7, 2010, http://www.nytimes.com/2010/02/08/world/asia/08iht-asiawomen.html.
5. Pico Iyer, "1986: Corazon Aquino," *Time*, January 5, 1987, http://www.time.com/time/subscriber/personoftheyear/archive/stories/1986.html.
6. "Corazon Aquino Speaks to Fulbrighters," Fulbright Association, http://www.fulbright.org/sites/default/files/Aquino%20Address.doc.
7. "Corazon Aquino Quotes," Corazon Aquino Infosite, http://corazonaquino.net/more.html.

Chapter 9: Be Tenacious
1. Jeremiah Farrell, ed., *Word Ways: The Journal of Recreational Linguistics*, http://wordways.com/panama.htm (article no longer available on website).
2. David McCullough, *The Path Between the Seas: The Creation of the Panama Canal, 1870–1914* (New York: Simon & Schuster, 1977), 610.
3. "Quotations from the Speeches and Other Works of Theodore Roosevelt," Theodore Roosevelt Association, http://www.theodoreroosevelt.org/life/quotes.htm.
4. Christopher Helman, "The Man Behind the Curtain," *Forbes*, November 8, 2010, http://www.forbes.com/forbes/2010/1108/anschutz-qwest-leiweke-bieber-staples-behind-curtain_2.html.

5. "Philip Anschutz," Horatio Alger Association, http://www
.horatioalger.com/members/member_info.cfm?memberid=ans00.
6. Jerry Clower, "You're on My List," *Greatest Hits,* MCA Nashville,
1994.
7. Ron Kurtus, "Winston Churchill's 'Never Give Up' Speech," Ron
Kurtus' School for Champions, http://www.school-for-champions
.com/speeches/churchill_never_give_in.htm.
8. Kurtus.

Chapter 10: Keep a Forgiving Spirit

1. Elisabeth Elliot, *Shadow of the Almighty: The Life and Testament of
Jim Elliot* (New York: Harper and Brothers, 1958), 88–89.
2. Elliot, 172.
3. Janet and Geoff Benge, *Jim Elliot: One Great Purpose* (Seattle:
YWAM Publishing, 1999), 100.
4. See Elisabeth Elliot, *Passion and Purity: Learning to Bring Your
Love Life Under Christ's Control* (Grand Rapids, MI: Revell, 2002).
5. The name of the Huaorani people is sometimes spelled Waodani
in English. Other variant spellings are occasionally found.
6. The story of Elisabeth's work with the Huaorani after Jim's death
is beautifully told in the motion pictures *End of the Spear* (directed
by Jim Hanon, Every Tribe Entertainment, 2005) and *Beyond the
Gates of Splendor* (directed by Jim Hanon, Bearing Fruit
Entertainment, 2002).
7. Stephen E. Saint, "The Unfinished Mission to the 'Aucas,'"
Christianity Today, March 2, 1998, http://www.christianitytoday
.com/ct/1998/march2/8t3042.html.
8. Galatians 6:7.
9. Luke 4:18; Romans 10:9-10.
10. Isaiah 53:4; Matthew 26:38.

Chapter 11: Keep a Positive Outlook

1. Obituary of Clement Stone, *New York Times*, September 5, 2002.
2. Obituary of Clement Stone.
3. Forrest Wallace Cato, "The Last Interview with Financial
Industry Legend: W. Clement Stone (May 4, 1902–September 3,
2002)," *The Register* 7, no. 8 (August 2006).
4. Teen Challenge Research, "Significant Research That Everybody
Should Know," Association of Christian Alcohol and Drug
Counselors Institute, http://www.acadc.org/page/page/2495014.htm.

5. "W. Clement Stone Quotes," BrainyQuote, http://www
.brainyquote.com/quotes/authors/w/w_clement_stone.html.
6. "Wham-Bam-Slam!" directed by Jules White, Columbia Short
Subjects, 1955.
7. Genesis 50:19-20, NIV.
8. Romans 8:28, NIV.
9. See Mark 12:30.
10. See Exodus 20:1-17.

Chapter 12: Using What You Have to Get What You Want
1. Jesse Wendell Castleberry and Rosalie Nieft Castleberry, *Castleberry and Allied Families*, vol. 1, Jesse Wendell Castleberry, 1966.
2. John 6:9-13.

ABOUT THE AUTHOR

JOSEPH CASTLEBERRY is president of Northwest University in Kirkland, Washington. His life story is the tale of dreams made real by God's guidance and provision. Educated at Evangel University, Princeton Theological Seminary, and Columbia University, he began ministry as a chaplain at Princeton University. He served as an educator, church planter, and community development leader in Latin America and as a seminary dean and university president in the United States. He speaks frequently at church conferences around the world. Best of all, he has been blessed with a happy marriage that has made him the proud father of three daughters.